EnglishSmart — Grammar 4

Contents

1. **Nouns** — Common & Proper Nouns • Noun Plurals • Collective Nouns ... 2
2. **Pronouns** — Personal Pronouns • Cases of Pronouns • Interrogative Pronouns ... 6
3. **Adjectives** — Comparative & Superlative Forms • Nouns as Adjectives ... 10
4. **Adverbs** — Forming Adverbs • Comparative & Superlative Forms • Irregular Adverbs ... 14
5. **Verbs** — Transitive & Intransitive Verbs • Auxiliary Verbs • Verb Forms ... 18
6. **The Sentence** — Subject & Predicate • Compound Subjects • Compound Verbs • Verb Agreement • Compound Sentences ... 22
7. **Building Sentences with Descriptors** — Adjective & Adverb Phrases • Verbal Phrases ... 26

Progress Test 1 ... 30

8. **Prepositions and Conjunctions** — Prepositional Phrases • Conjunctions • Subordinating Conjunctions ... 36
9. **Building Complex Sentences** — Dependent & Independent Clauses • Forming Complex Sentences with Conjunctions • Using Verbals ... 40
10. **Relative Clauses** — The Restrictive Relative Clauses • The Non-Restrictive Relative Clauses ... 44
11. **Developing the Paragraph** — Topic Sentences • Body Sentences • Conclusions • Writing Short Paragraphs ... 48
12. **Rules of Punctuation** — End Punctuation • Abbreviations • Commas • Apostrophes • Quotation Marks ... 52
13. **Punctuation, Capitalization, and Abbreviations** — Semicolons • Colons • Capitalization • Abbreviations ... 56
14. **Tips for Effective Writing** — Subject-Verb Agreement • Choppy Sentences • Punctuation Errors • Confusing Homonyms • Double Negatives ... 60
15. **Writing Descriptive and Narrative Paragraphs** — Descriptive Paragraphs • Narrative Paragraphs ... 64

Progress Test 2 ... 68

Answers ... 75

1 Nouns

A **Noun** is a word that represents a person, place, or thing. Nouns can be either Common or Proper.

Examples: Bicycle, dog, house, gymnasium, father, and child are all **Common Nouns**. They refer to **non-specific** persons, places, or things, and often represent a group or a classification.

Exercise A

In each group of words below, circle the one that is <u>not</u> a common noun.

1. book   jumps   window   cake
2. bulky   height   weight   size
3. television   camera   sings   performance
4. baseball   team   exciting   coach
5. tools   hammer   useful   nail
6. children   happy   school   classroom

Proper Nouns refer to **specific** persons, places, or things, and require capitalization.
Examples: Ford Explorer, Glen Road Public School, and Terry Fox are all **Proper Nouns** because they refer to **specific** persons, places, or things. Notice that these nouns begin with capital letters.

Exercise B

Identify the proper noun in each group below and capitalize its first letter.

1. harry potter   author   story   character
2. player   teammate   joe sakic   winger
3. opera   theatre   cn tower   stadium
4. bank   royal bank   teller   money
5. arena   air canada centre   rink   ice
6. amusement park   wonderland   circus   clowns

Underline both the common and proper nouns in the following sentences. Capitalize the proper nouns.

Do not include pronouns in your selections.

1. ramon gonzales and his sister, julia, attend williamson road public school.

2. They enjoy playing sports at recess time.

3. ramon is a very good basketball player while julia prefers to play volleyball.

4. The gonzales family moved to canada from spain three years ago and live in a downtown neighbourhood.

5. julia and ramon speak both spanish and english and are learning french in school.

6. mr. gonzales works as a computer programmer and mrs. gonzales is an interior decorator.

7. In the gonzales family there are four children, but only two of the children attend school.

8. Next summer, the family will visit their cousins in spain.

Noun Plurals

Here are five basic rules for making nouns plural; however, there are many exceptions to these rules.

Rule 1: Most nouns form the plural by simply adding **s** to the singular nouns.
Examples: car – cars   bicycle – bicycles   boy – boys   girl – girls

Rule 2: Nouns ending in **f** or **fe**
In some cases add **s** to the original nouns.
Examples: chief – chiefs   giraffe – giraffes

For most nouns ending in **f** or **fe**, change the **f** to **v** and add **es**.
Examples: life – lives   wife – wives

Rule 3: Nouns ending in **s** or **sh**, **ch**, **x**, and **z**
Add **es** to the singular noun (if proper pronunciation requires the extra syllable).
Examples: wax – waxes   business – businesses

Rule 4: a. If a consonant comes before the **y**, change the **y** to **i** and add **es**.
b. If a vowel comes before the **y**, then simply add **s**.
Examples: army – armies   city – cities   but   key – keys and valley – valleys

Rule 5: a. If a vowel comes before the **o** ending, in most cases add **s**.
b. If a consonant comes before the **o** ending, in most cases add **es**.
Examples: rodeo – rodeos   but   hero – heroes

Exercise D

Change the following nouns to plural form. Check the rules above if you are not sure of the proper ending. Enter the Rule # that fits each change.

1. army _____ Rule # ____   2. lunch _____ Rule # ____

3. pen _____ Rule # ____   4. duty _____ Rule # ____

5. proof _____ Rule # ____   6. lady _____ Rule # ____

7. life _____ Rule # ____   8. journey _____ Rule # ____

9. half _____ Rule # ____   10. patio _____ Rule # ____

11. tax _____ Rule # ____   12. radio _____ Rule # ____

13. car _____ Rule # ____   14. diary _____ Rule # ____

15. church _____ Rule # ____   16. leaf _____ Rule # ____

CHALLENGE

1. What do these nouns have in common?
   sheep   deer   moose   salmon   grass   aircraft

   Answer: _____

2. Write the plural form of the nouns below. They change completely and do not follow any rules.

   A. ox _____   B. mouse _____
   C. child _____   D. tooth _____

Collective Nouns are singular but refer to groups of people or things.
Example: "Orchestra" is a singular noun but refers to a number of musicians.

Exercise E

Complete the Collective Noun Crossword Puzzle.

Down

A. workers on a boat
B. all the players together
C. a group or a club
D. a group of soldiers
E. soldiers on the sea

Across

1. a country
2. a business
3. people gathering together

1. n _ t _ _ n
2. c _ m a _ y
3. c _ _ w

2 Pronouns

A **Pronoun** is used in place of a noun. It refers to a person, place, or thing without naming it. It must agree in gender (male or female) and number (singular or plural) with the noun it is replacing.

Personal Pronouns
Singular: I   you   he   she   it   one   me   him   her
Plural: we   you   they   ones   us   them
Possessive: my   mine   our   ours   your   yours   his   her   hers   its   one's   their   theirs

Note: The noun that is being replaced by the pronoun is called its **Antecedent**.

Exercise A

Fill in each blank with the proper pronoun. Choose pronouns from the ones listed above.

> Make sure your choice of pronoun agrees with the verb, the antecedent noun in the sentences, or the other pronoun being used.

1. Paul's bicycle broke down so _____ needed repair.

2. The students brought _____ pets to school.

3. Shakira invited all the students to _____ birthday party.

4. The teacher asked _____ to show our homework.

5. At lunchtime the students often shared _____ treats.

6. Recess was a time for _____ to play our favourite games.

7. Our favourite game in the spring was baseball because _____ could be played with many participants.

8. _____ chose our teams for the baseball game by a random draw.

9. He asked _____ a question that I could not answer.

10. When the teacher asked who owned the binder that was found in the yard, Amanda realized that it was _____ .

An **Objective Pronoun** is either the receiver of the action of the verb or the object of a preposition.

Example (1): He tripped him during the race.
"He" is a nominative pronoun, subject of the verb "tripped".
"Him" is an objective pronoun because it is the object of the sentence and receives the action of the verb.

Example (2): He gave the prize to him for winning the race.
"He" is a nominative pronoun, subject of the verb "gave".
"Him" is the object of the preposition "to" and therefore takes the objective case.

Exercise B

Place the proper case of pronoun in the space provided for each sentence.

1. We received a message from _____ (them, they).

2. She gave _____ (we, us) a phone call.

3. To _____ (who, whom) are you speaking?

4. The teacher gave _____ (her, she) an award.

5. The player passed the ball to _____ (him, he).

6. Please let _____ (me, I) join in your game.

7. The teacher asked to speak to _____ (she, her) in private.

A **Possessive Pronoun** shows ownership. There are singular and plural forms of possession for a pronoun.

Exercise C

Place the correct possessive form of the pronoun in each sentence.

1. She brought _____ dog to school.

2. John plays _____ guitar every night.

3. The students in grade four have _____ own playground.

4. We enjoyed _____ vacation.

5. You have found _____ but I have lost _____ .

 **Interrogative Pronouns** ask questions. **Who, What, Which, Whose** are examples of interrogative pronouns.

Exercise D

In the blanks, place the proper interrogative pronoun. Place a different pronoun for each blank space.

1. _____ of the ice cream flavours is your favourite?
2. _____ books did you borrow for summer reading?
3. _____ is knocking at the door?
4. _____ are you planning to go for your vacation?

Exercise E

Fill in each space with the proper case of pronoun to suit the antecedent noun.

> Make sure the pronoun also agrees with the verb in the sentence.

The Class Trip

On Thursday the grade four class was scheduled to go on a school trip to the zoo. 1._____ (it, we) was located on the other side of the city. 2._____ (they, we) were asked to bring 3._____ (her, their) own lunch. 4._____ (theirs, their) teacher, Ms. Renaldo, asked each of 5._____ (they, them) to bring a notebook and a pen to write down facts about the animals. John lost his bus tickets so Ms. Renaldo gave 6._____ (her, him) two more of 7._____ (these, them). When 8._____ (they, you)

arrived, the students formed a line at the entrance to meet 9._____ (your, their) guide for the day. 10._____ (her, his) name was Peter and 11._____ (our, he) took 12._____ (us, them) to the African section first. The lions were asleep in 13._____ (theirs, their) den. The monkeys playfully swung among branches and seemed to want to entertain the students. 14._____ (they, it) even made faces at 15._____ (he, them) when 16._____ (they, us) got close to the fence. The teacher asked jokingly to 17._____ (whom, who) the monkeys were speaking.

CHALLENGE

Circle the pronoun in each sentence from both Column A and Column B. The pronoun in each of these sentences is wrong. Make a trade with a pronoun from the other column.

Be careful – there is only one match for each sentence.

The Pronoun Switch Game

Column A

1. John tied her shoe.
2. The boys kept the candy to ourselves.
3. John wasn't sure to who he should call.
4. The audience clapped our hands.
5. We took my time getting here.

Column B

a. We helped themselves to the treats.
b. Whom is at the door?
c. Cheryl hurt his foot.
d. I walked home on our own.
e. We raised their voices in the singing.

3 Adjectives

An **Adjective** is used to modify or describe a noun or a pronoun. It gives additional information about a noun such as its size, colour, shape, number, or type.

Examples: the **green** car, the **large** house, the **round** swimming pool, the **three** boys, the **professional** player, the **other** book, the **school** yard

Do not confuse adjectives and adverbs. Remember, an adverb modifies a verb – the action word – in a sentence.

Exercise A

Underline the adjectives in each of the following sentences. The number in parentheses ( ) after each sentence tells you the number of adjectives in the sentence.

1. The tall boy threw his baseball through the small window. (3)

2. The cold rain pelted down on the tired fishermen. (2)

3. When the snow was deep, the older children built huge snow forts. (4)

4. Thousands of bright stars lit up the dark sky. (2)

5. This adventure story is a favourite of the younger children. (3)

6. The little girls played a short but sweet melody. (3)

The **Comparative** form of an adjective is used to compare two nouns. To change an adjective to the comparative form, add **er** to the original (descriptive) adjective.
Example: John is tall**er** than Paul.

The **Superlative** form of an adjective is used to compare more than two nouns. To change the original (descriptive) adjective to the superlative form, add **est**.
Example: John is the tall**est** boy in his class.

If an adjective ends in a single consonant, double the final consonant and add "er", e.g. thin – thinner. If an adjective ends in a double consonant, just add "er", e.g. smart – smarter. If an adjective ends in a "y", change the "y" to "i" and add "er", e.g. juicy – juicier.

10 EnglishSmart – Grammar • Grade 4

Exercise B

Fill in the chart with the comparative and superlative forms of the simple adjectives listed.

	Simple	Comparative	Superlative
1.	small		smallest
2.	early	earlier	
3.	happy		
4.	sad		
5.	cheap		
6.	fine		
7.	kind		
8.	new		

Some adjectives do not follow the rules above for changing to the comparative and superlative forms.

Exercise C

Complete the chart using the comparative and superlative forms.

Use some of the given adjectives more than once in the chart below.

worse   less   more
most   worst   best   good
more   some   least

	Simple	Comparative	Superlative
1.		better	
2.	much		
3.	bad		
4.			most
5.	little		

EnglishSmart – Grammar • **Grade 4** 11

 For many **adjectives with two or more syllables**, we place "more" or "less" before the simple adjective when comparing two things.

Examples: Her dog was **more intelligent** than mine.
He was the **less tired** of the two runners.

For the superlative form, "most" or "least" may be added to the adjective.
Examples: They watched the **most exciting** game.
This was the **least difficult** of the questions.

Exercise D

Circle the proper comparative or superlative form for each adjective below.

1. healthy   a. healthier   b. more healthier
2. beautiful   a. beautifullest   b. most beautiful
3. smart   a. smarter   b. more smarter
4. interesting   a. more interesting   b. interestinger
5. nice   a. nicest   b. most nice
6. happy   a. less happiest   b. least happy

 **Nouns as Adjectives**
Sometimes a noun will be used like an adjective to modify (describe) another noun.
Example: chicken soup
The word "chicken" is a noun but it is acting as an adjective because it describes the kind of soup.

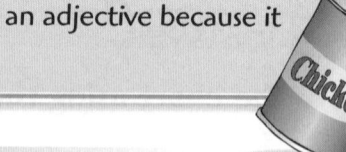

Exercise E

Match each noun/adjective in Column A with the noun it could describe.

Column A   **Column B**

1. New York   (   )   A. programme
2. space   (   )   B. team
3. movie   (   )   C. star
4. chocolate   (   )   D. station
5. school   (   )   E. sundae
6. family   (   )   F. City
7. television (   )   G. yard
8. football   (   )   H. member

Exercise F

Fill in the blanks with adjectives selected from the words below that make sense in the sentences.

Read all the words first; cross them off as you use them.

spacious   bus   cool   wise   hottest   No Swimming
disappointed   most   public   local

A Day at the Beach

Because it was the 1._____ day of the year, the camp counsellors made the 2._____ decision to go to the 3._____ beach. They gave each camper a 4._____ ticket for the trip. The campers were 5._____ anxious to jump into the 6._____ lake water. However, when they arrived there was a 7._____ sign posted. The 8._____ campers thought that they would have to go back to the camp. Luckily, there was a 9._____ swimming pool nearby. Soon all the campers were cooling off in the 10._____ swimming pool.

4 Adverbs

An **Adverb** is a word that describes (modifies) a verb (action word).
An adverb can also modify an adjective and another adverb in a sentence.
Adverbs answer the questions "where", "when", "how", and "how much".
Adverbs often end in "ly".

Exercise A

Underline the adverbs in the following sentences. Indicate in the space provided whether the adverbs describe where, when, how, or how much.

1. The boys swam <u>swiftly</u>.   how

2. The girl spoke loudly so that everyone could hear her.   _____

3. It always rains when we have a baseball game.   _____

4. The teacher asked the students to come quickly to the gymnasium.   _____

5. He walked slowly down the street.   _____

6. He soon arrived home.   _____

7. The student spoke sincerely about her family.   _____

8. He shot the puck accurately at the net and quickly scored a goal.   _____ _____

9. The students worked busily at their history assignment.   _____

10. The older boy ran faster than the younger boy who ran farther.   _____ _____

11. The player was slightly hurt when the ball hit him.   _____

Forming Adverbs
Adverbs can be formed by adding "ly" or "ily" to a word.
Examples: greed – greed**ily**   happy – happ**ily**   sad – sad**ly**
If the original word ends in "y", drop the "y" and add "ily" to change that word to an adverb.
Example: happy – happ**ily**

Exercise B

Change the following words to adverbs. Place the adverb form in the space provided.

1. entire _____
2. greedy _____
3. fair _____
4. simple _____
5. sloppy _____
6. happy _____
7. desperate _____
8. nice _____
9. silent _____
10. weary _____

In some cases an adverb will modify an adjective instead of modifying a verb (action word).
Example: He was **pleasantly tired** after the workout.
"Pleasantly" is an adverb modifying the adjective "tired".
An adverb can also modify another adverb.
Example: He played **remarkably** well.
"Remarkably" is an adverb modifying the adverb "well".

Exercise C

Underline the adverbs that are modifying adjectives and other adverbs in the sentences below. Place parentheses ( ) around the adjectives or adverbs being modified.

1. The boat drifted lazily along.
2. The candy was sickly sweet.
3. The campers woke incredibly early.
4. The students were not entirely pleased with their test results.
5. The desperately hungry boy ate a huge lunch.
6. It was a fairly dark night.
7. The badly injured athlete was carried off the field.
8. The completely useless tool was thrown away.

To form a **Comparative Adverb**, place the word "more" before the adverb; to form the **Superlative** form of an adverb, place the word "most" before the adverb.

Examples: He writes clearly. He writes **more clearly** than his friend writes.
They treated us kindly. They treated us **most kindly**.

Exercise D

Rewrite the sentences below using the appropriate adverb form.

1. He rides his bicycle carefully than his brother.
   _____

2. He played hockey skilfully than all his team-mates.
   _____

3. The dogs in the cage barked viciously than the dogs on leashes.
   _____

4. The librarian spoke enthusiastically than our teacher about the book.
   _____

5. Her homework was carefully done than mine.
   _____

Some **Irregular Adverbs** change completely when becoming either comparative or superlative in form.
Examples: He swims **well**. He swims **better**. He swims **best**.

Exercise E

Fill in the blanks with the proper comparative and superlative forms of the following adverbs. Choose the correct words from the list below.

worse   better   best   worst

Adverb	Comparative	Superlative
1. bad		
2. well		
3. badly		

Exercise F

Fill in the blanks with the suitable adverbs provided.

Some blanks may require comparative or superlative adverb forms.

A Day at the Baseball Game

generously   kindly
wildly   dangerously
easily   vigorously
excitedly   finally
incredibly

We 1._____ hopped into the car to go to the Saturday afternoon baseball game at the SkyDome. When we 2._____ arrived, the Toronto Blue Jays were 3._____ warming up on the field before the game. The usher 4._____ allowed us to ask for autographs. Most players offered 5._____ to sign our programmes. When the players took the field to begin the game, we cheered 6._____ . The first batter avoided a pitch that was 7._____ close to his head. Then, with a sudden explosive swing, he drove the ball 8._____ out of the park. The Blue Jays went on to win 9._____ over the opposition.

5 Verbs

A **Verb** is a word or group of words that shows the action in a sentence. It is the action performed by the subject (or object) of a sentence.

Examples: Paul **runs** across the street.
They **sailed** around the lake.
The people **were gathering** in front of the bus stop.

Exercise A

The number following each sentence tells you how many verbs are in it.

Underline the verbs in the following sentences.

1. The children were playing in the park. (1)
2. The school principal made an announcement over the P.A. system. (1)
3. When he arrived home, he phoned a friend. (2)
4. The school bell rang loudly and the students began to line up. (2)
5. The dogs ran around the yard while the cat sat in the window and watched. (3)

A **Transitive Verb** is an action word that requires an object. An object is the receiver of the action of the verb.

Example: The girl **carried** her books.

The word "carried" is the verb and the word "books" is the object of the verb, that is, the thing that is being carried.

An **Intransitive Verb** does not require an object to complete its meaning.

Examples: She **laughed** at the joke.
He **rowed** across the river.

Exercise B

In each of the following sentences, underline the transitive verbs and place parentheses ( ) around the objects that receive the action of these verbs.

1. The parents applauded the performance of the play.
2. He shot the puck into the net.

3. The girls in the class sang a song while the boys performed a dance.
4. The bus driver took the passengers' tickets before leaving the depot.
5. The children played baseball in the schoolyard while the teachers held a meeting.

Exercise C

Place "T" for transitive and "I" for intransitive after each sentence. Underline the verb in each sentence.

1. The coach asked the players to try harder. _____
2. Don't ask questions. _____
3. The night sky was bright with stars. _____
4. The horses raced around the track. _____
5. He played a new game on his computer. _____

Auxiliary Verbs help the main verbs in a sentence. The following words are often used as auxiliary verbs: may, be, shall, will, might, must, have, has, and can.

Examples: She **may** eat her dinner in the living room.
The boys **will** play hockey after school.
Everyone **has** been helpful.
She **has** walked all the way home.

Exercise D

Write the proper auxiliary verb in each space provided.

1. The young girl _____ (will, was) help her mother when she needs it.

2. The ocean tide _____ (have, has) moved farther out.

3. He _____ (did, will) go to the game if he can get a ticket.

4. The students _____ (must, might) obey the rules of the school to avoid getting into trouble.

5. They _____ (have, will) take a trip if they can get time off work.

Parts of a Verb

In English there are four main parts of most verbs: present, present participle, past, past participle.

The **present tense** (form) of the verb is the basic form.

The **past tense** is the form that shows that the action of the verb has already occurred. The past tense is usually formed by adding "ed" or "d" to the basic form.

The **present participle** form of a verb is formed by adding "ing" to the basic verb.

The **past participle** may have the same form as that of the past tense.

Examples: present tense – cross, do, go, walk
present participle – crossing, doing, going, walking
past tense – crossed, did, went, walked
past participle – crossed, done, gone, walked

Note: The verb "go" is irregular and its past tense form is "went".

Exercise E

The past participle and the past tense are often the same.

Fill in the proper form of the verbs in the chart that match the form provided. The first one is done for you.

Basic Form	Past Tense	Present Participle	Past Participle
1. begin	began	beginning	begun
2. catch			
3.		cutting	
4. become			
5. draw			drawn
6.		knowing	
7.	heard		
8. read			
9.		wearing	
10.	wrote		
11.		going	
12. bite			
13.			sung

Exercise F

Place the proper form of the verb in parentheses ( ) in the space provided for each sentence below.

1. The athletes from our school _____ (was, were) gathering in front of the school to _____ (organize, organized) themselves for the track and field competition.

2. After the bus had _____ (arrive, arrived), we were finally on our way.

3. When our athletes _____ (arriving, arrived) at the stadium, many teams _____ (have, had) been _____ (prepare, preparing) for the events.

4. Our 200-metre runner, Paul, _____ (feel, felt) that he had a good chance to win his race.

5. Our school had _____ (training, trained) very hard for this competition.

6. Our relay team was _____ (running, ran) in the inside lane.

7. Paul _____ (comes, came) second in the 200-metre race, and our relay team had _____ (placing, placed) first.

8. Everyone was very proud of the victory, and the relay team _____ (ran, running) a victory lap around the track.

9. When it was time for the 100-metre race, the runners were _____ (taken, taking) their marks _____ (waited, waiting) for the gun to go off.

10. After a fierce race, our runner _____ (finished, finishing) third.

6 The Sentence

A **Sentence** is a group of words that expresses a complete thought.
A **Simple Sentence** is made up of a subject and a predicate. The subject (usually a noun) performs an action; the predicate, which includes a verb, describes the action.

Example: The boy | threw the ball to his friend.
 subject – the boy   bare subject (noun) – boy
 predicate – threw the ball to his friend   bare predicate (verb) – threw

Exercise A

For each sentence below draw a line separating the subject and predicate, and draw a line under the bare subject (noun) and the bare predicate (verb).

Straight   *a wavy line under*

1. John watched a movie with his friends.
2. The tired travellers waited at the bus terminal.
3. Most swimmers fear the presence of sharks.
4. Canada is the largest country in the world.
5. He will take his bicycle with him on holiday.
6. It is a beautiful day today.

Compound Subjects and Compound Verbs
In a simple sentence it is possible to have two or more subjects (compound) and two or more verbs.

Example (1): **Peter and Paul** are brothers.
 The compound subjects are joined by the conjunction "and".

Example (2): The puppy | likes to **run and jump** around the yard.
 The compound verbs are joined by the conjunction "and".

Exercise B

Unscramble each group of words below to form sentences with a compound subject, a compound verb, or both.

1. horses   barn   shared   the   and   cows   the

_____

22 EnglishSmart – Grammar • Grade 4

2. cried   time   the   same   she   and   at   laughed
_____

3. red   and   are   favourite   colours   her   blue   yellow
_____

4. chewed   his   swallowed   food   he   and   digested
_____

5. carried   the   packed   and   boxes   girls   the   boys   and
_____

6. or   Maria   babysit   tonight   Joanna   will
_____

7. clothes   Janet   this   washed   the   morning   dried   and
_____

8. see   hens   some   I   and   there   can   over   ducks
_____

> **Verb Agreement**
> In a sentence, the subject and verb must agree. A single subject requires the singular form of the verb; a compound subject requires the plural form of the verb.
> **Examples:** His <u>mother</u> **is** working late tonight. (singular)
> His <u>mother</u> and <u>father</u> **are** working late tonight. (plural)

Exercise C

In each sentence, change the verb in parentheses ( ) to match the subject.

1. She _____ (have) a new car.
2. John and Peter _____ (likes) to play hockey.
3. Eric _____ (want) to buy a new pair of running shoes.
4. Susan, Ashley, and Dayna _____ (is) in the same class.
5. Lauren and Kara _____ (was) the last to leave the party.
6. Children _____ (plays) in the schoolyard.
7. Jessica and I _____ (am) good friends.

When two simple sentences are joined together with a conjunction (and, or, but, if...), then a **Compound Sentence** is formed.

Example: The children were caught in the rain and they didn't have umbrellas.
Note the joining word (conjunction) "and" which joins the two simple sentences.

Exercise D

Match the sentences in Column A with those in Column B forming compound sentences that make sense. Write the compound sentence that you have formed by connecting the sentences with a joining word (conjunction).

so   if   and   but

Column A

1. School was cancelled
2. It was her birthday
3. The weather was awful
4. We would be rewarded with treats
5. The fishermen waited patiently
6. They will be late
7. The children played a vigorous game of soccer
8. The boys were hungry

Column B

- they didn't catch a thing
- they miss the train
- we played outside anyway
- the students went home
- there was nothing for them to eat
- she opened her presents
- they were all very tired
- we did all our work

1. _____
2. _____
3. _____
4. _____
5. _____
6. _____
7. _____
8. _____

Incomplete Sentences

A sentence must convey a complete thought in order for it to make sense to the reader.

Example: When I was walking home

This is not a complete sentence because it needs more information for it to make sense.

When I was walking home, I met my friend, Kyle.

Notice that with the additional information – "I met my friend Kyle" – the sentence now makes sense.

Incomplete sentences such as the one in the example above are called **Fragments**.

Exercise E

Imagine that you are either a spectator at the school play or one of the actors in the play. Complete the sentences below telling a story about your experience with the school play.

The School Play

1. When the curtain went up, _____

2. During the first scene, _____

3. _____ because the costumes were too warm.

4. _____ when the lights went dim.

5. If you forget your lines, _____

6. Because it was the first school play, _____

7. _____ even after many rehearsals.

8. Although some people were nervous, _____

9. When the play was finished, _____

7 Building Sentences with Descriptors

The basic sentence is made up of two parts: a subject and a predicate.
To make a sentence more interesting and to add important information to a sentence, descriptors can be added.
Descriptors include adjectives, adverbs, adjective phrases, and adverb phrases.
Example: Here is a basic sentence with a subject and a predicate.
The girl ran home.
Here is the same sentence with an adjective and an adverb.
The **happy** girl ran home **quickly**.

Exercise A

Make each of the following sentences more interesting by adding an adjective to describe the subject and an adverb to describe the verb. Choose from the adjective/adverb word pairs to fill in the blanks in each sentence below.

Use both words in each pair for each sentence below.

puffy, lazily   hot, mercilessly   French, quietly
brave, fearlessly   young, gracefully   best, kindly
vicious, fiercely   reckless, dangerously

1. The _____ teacher _____ called out our names.
2. His _____ dog barked _____ at the people passing by.
3. The _____ clouds drifted _____ overhead.
4. The _____ sun beat down _____ on the sunbathers.
5. The _____ ballerina danced _____ on the stage.
6. The _____ stuntman jumped _____ from the top of the building.
7. The _____ firefighter _____ entered the burning building.
8. Her _____ friend _____ offered to help her clean her room.

26 EnglishSmart – Grammar • Grade 4

A **Phrase** is a group of words that acts as a single word in a sentence. Unlike sentences and clauses, phrases do not contain a subject and a predicate.

An **Adjective Phrase** acts as an adjective and describes a noun.

Example: The hat in the box was a gift for his mother.
"In the box" is an adjective phrase because it gives information about the hat.

An **Adverb Phrase** acts as an adverb and describes a verb.

Example: He placed his mother's hat in the box.
"In the box" is an adverb phrase because it tells where the hat was placed.

Adverb phrases often answer the questions where and when.

Exercise B

In the space following each sentence, write "ADV" (adverb) or "ADJ" (adjective) to indicate which type of phrase is used. Underline the preposition that introduces each phrase.

1. The children played *in the school yard* during recess. _____

2. They played a game *of baseball* called "workups". _____

3. Their game was interrupted by the ringing *of the bell*. _____

4. The team *with the most runs* when the bell rang was the winner. _____

5. John is the best baseball player *in our school*. _____

6. He once hit the ball *over the schoolyard fence*. _____

7. Mr. Wright, the grade four teacher, picks even teams *of twelve players*. _____

8. He said that one day we could play a team *from another school*. _____

9. He said that the game would take place *at the community baseball diamond*. _____

10. We are hoping to arrange to play this game *in the spring*. _____

Exercise C

Underline the phrases in the sentences below. Sometimes one phrase follows another.

There are 16 phrases in the 10 sentences below, but one sentence does not have a phrase at all!

1. They rode their bikes across the field and over the hill.
2. In the summertime, his family rents a cottage by a small lake.
3. If the teacher asks a question, he will give the answer in the textbook.
4. At the beginning of our gym class, the teacher checks our uniforms.
5. He stood up in front of the class and read a poem.
6. After we ate lunch, we organized games in the gymnasium.
7. We placed our books under our desks during the test.
8. Our umbrellas were useful when the rain came down.
9. We let the dog in the house because it was cold in the doghouse.
10. The campers pitched their tents in the clearing and cooked supper on the campfire.

Exercise D

Create a descriptive paragraph by using as many of the phrases given below as possible. Add your own descriptive phrases to the sentences that you are composing.

Perhaps you could organize your sentences in a rough draft first.

A Daytrip to the Beach

in the sand   in the car   on Lake Ontario   with my family
in the water   after our picnic   during the drive home
at the gas station   to the beach   on a daytrip
in the hot sun   after breakfast   on July 22

_____

_____

_____
_____
_____
_____
_____
_____

Verbal Phrases begin with the participle form of a verb which ends in "ing". Skiing, running, jumping, singing are all verbals.

When a verbal is used as a noun, it is called a gerund.

Example: **Skiing** is her favourite sport.

When a verbal involves a group of words, it becomes a verbal phrase.

Example: **Skiing in the mountains** is her favourite activity.

CHALLENGE

At the beginning of each sentence below is a verbal. Add words to that verbal to make a verbal phrase and a complete sentence.

1. Swimming ____in cool water____ is refreshing.
2. Laughing _____ is not polite.
3. Singing _____ is her after-school activity.
4. Throwing _____ with a partner is fun.
5. Running _____ is their everyday exercise.
6. Playing _____ is a favourite of school children.
7. Enjoying _____ is a good family activity.
8. Exercising _____ is good for your health.
9. Helping _____ is a nice thing to do.

EnglishSmart – Grammar • **Grade 4**

Progress Test 1

Nouns

Exercise A

There may be more than one noun in each row.

Circle the nouns in each row of words below.

1. walking   sidewalk   walked   waking   walker
2. glad   happy   sad   sadness   happiness
3. before   after   afternoon   morning   mourn
4. children   childish   childlike   infant   child
5. unusual   strange   stranger   weird   different

Exercise B

Underline the proper nouns in each row below.

There may be more than one proper noun in each row. Capital letters have been removed from the proper nouns for test purposes.

1. mount everest   mountains   mountainous   location
2. john   boy   friend   classmate
3. june   month   date   july
4. ottawa   ottawa river   riverbank   ocean
5. disneyland   studio   amusement park   recreation
6. hockey   the toronto maple leafs   professionals   nhl

Exercise C

Write the plural or singular form of each noun in the space.

Singular	Plural
1.	oxen
2. mouse	
3. fish	
4.	children

Singular	Plural
5. wife	
6. life	
7. tooth	
8.	feet

Pronouns

Exercise D

Write the possessive form, the plural form, and the possessive form of the plural for each pronoun.

	Pronoun	Possessive	Plural	Possessive
1.	I			
2.	she			
3.	it			
4.	you			

Adjectives

Exercise E

Circle the adjective form in each row of words below.

1. beauty   beautiful   beautify
2. wear   weary   wearing
3. care   careful   careless
4. large   big   enormous
5. gold   golden   bracelet
6. precious   valuable   diamond

There may be more than one adjective form in each row.

Exercise F

Underline the proper comparative or superlative form for each adjective below.

1. large ⟶ a. most larger   b. more larger   c. larger
2. huge ⟶ a. hugest   b. most hugest   c. most huger
3. lucky ⟶ a. luckier   b. more luckiest   c. luckierest
4. fine ⟶ a. most finer   b. more finest   c. finest
5. bad   ⟶ a. worse   b. more badder   c. baddest

Progress Test 1

Adverbs

Exercise G

Underline the adverb form in each row below.

1. happy   happily   happiness
2. careless   careful   carelessly
3. quickly   quickness   quick
4. creative   creatively   creation
5. final   finished   finally

Verbs

Exercise H

Three sentences below have two verbs.

Underline the verb in each sentence below.

1. The boys chased after the dog that picked up their ball.
2. The rain poured down on the parade.
3. You laughed at the joke but it wasn't funny.
4. Richard and Michael ate their lunches and drank their milk in the park.
5. Swimming and running are good exercises.

Exercise I

Underline the verb(s) in each sentence and write "T" for transitive and "I" for intransitive in the spaces provided.

Transitive verbs require an object – a receiver of the action of the verb. Intransitive verbs do not require an object to complete the meaning of a sentence.

1. The Toronto Maple Leafs play in the Air Canada Centre.   ____
2. She chose the dress that she would wear for her birthday party.   ____ ____
3. The teacher gave us a talk about caring about the feelings of others.   ____
4. When he was speaking, we listened attentively.   ____ ____
5. The clouds covered the sky while the wind blew.   ____ ____

Exercise J

From the choices for each sentence, write the appropriate auxiliary (helping) verb in the space provided.

1. We _____ (will, were) walking home together after school.
2. The boat _____ (have, had) drifted out to the middle of the lake.
3. They _____ (could, have) take a trip this summer.
4. The children _____ (must, has) eat their lunch in the cafeteria.
5. She _____ (will, had) play after school tomorrow.

Exercise K

Write the appropriate past tense for each verb below in the space provided.

1. draw _____
2. see _____
3. catch _____
4. write _____
5. think _____
6. read _____
7. drive _____
8. has _____
9. do _____
10. cry _____

Sentences

Exercise L

Draw a line between the subject and the predicate of each sentence below. Underline the bare subject and the bare predicate in each sentence.

1. The team played football in the old stadium beside the river.
2. Both the boys and the girls used the same playing field during recess.
3. The audience laughed when they watched the funny movie.
4. We wear our gloves whenever it gets very cold.
5. The tall boys played basketball after school.
6. It rains whenever we plan a picnic.

Progress Test 1

Exercise M

The following sentences have either compound subjects, compound verbs, or both. Unscramble the sentences and underline the compound subjects and verbs.

1. and Mike Janet laughed sang and

   _____

2. game we baseball ate the peanuts popcorn and at

   _____

3. at same the laughed we and cried time

   _____

4. created presented they and together project the

   _____

5. jumped water the children in splashed and the

   _____

Exercise N

Change the verb in parentheses ( ) to agree with the subject in each of the sentences below. Put the correct verb in the space provided.

1. Paul _____ (want) to be the captain of the team.

2. Most of the students _____ (enjoys) creating artwork.

3. They _____ (carrying) their report cards home in envelopes.

4. Can't we _____ (gone) to the movies on Sunday afternoon?

5. Lucy _____ (giggling) too often in class, and the teacher _____ (are) not pleased.

6. Linda and Karen _____ (driven) to the store to shop for groceries.

7. Sam's uncle always _____ (make) funny jokes.

8. The drive to the cottage _____ (take) about two hours.

Adjective and Adverb Phrases

Exercise O

Underline the phrase in each sentence below and write "ADV" or "ADJ" in the space provided. If the sentence has more than one phrase, underline both and state the type of phrase in the order that they appear in the sentence.

> Each of these types of phrases begins with a preposition such as in, of, at, under, below, and before.

1. The door of the house was left open in the morning. _____ _____
2. Outside the window, a Blue Jay landed on a branch. _____ _____
3. In the evening, we went for a drive to town. _____ _____ _____
4. The car in the parking lot received a ticket. _____
5. The students of grade four were playing in the gymnasium. _____ _____
6. At the bottom of the pool sat the goggles of the polo player. _____ _____ _____

Exercise P

Underline the gerunds or verbal phrases in the sentences below. Write "G" for gerund or "VP" for verbal phrase in the space following each sentence.

> #3, 4, and 6 have either two gerunds or verbal phrases or one of each.

1. Swimming is my favourite summer activity. _____
2. Hiking in the mountains can be adventurous. _____
3. Looking in store windows can be interesting and cheaper than spending money. _____ _____
4. Singing and dancing are skills needed to be in the school play. _____ _____
5. I enjoy walking in the rain. _____
6. Skiing is fun but tobogganing down the hills is more exciting. _____ _____

EnglishSmart – Grammar • Grade 4   35

8 Prepositions and Conjunctions

A **Preposition** is a word that connects nouns and pronouns to other parts of a sentence.
A **Phrase** is a group of words that describes a noun or a verb. Phrases begin with prepositions.

Example: He placed his book **in** the desk.

"In" is a preposition that introduces the phrase "in the desk". The phrase tells us where the book is placed.

Can you pick out the prepositions in the sentences below? Underline the prepositions in each sentence.

1. The students went <u>to</u> the gym <u>after</u> school.
2. He placed his feet under the table.
3. The child went down the slide.
4. He slept during the movie.
5. They swam across the lake.
6. He was a cousin of mine.
7. He had to choose between cookies and cake.
8. The park was near the bus stop.
9. She did her homework without any help.
10. He waited inside the house for the rain to stop.

The first one is done for you.

Exercise B

Below are some common prepositions. Use each one in your own sentence.

| about | behind | onto | over | except | through |

1. _____
2. _____

3. _____
4. _____
5. _____
6. _____

> **Prepositional Phrases**
>
> Often a preposition is followed by a noun or pronoun. We refer to that noun or pronoun as the **object** of the preposition.
>
> A phrase that connects to a noun is an adjective phrase because, like an adjective, it describes that noun.
>
> A phrase that connects to a verb is an adverb phrase because it modifies the verb it is connected to.
>
> *Example:* The dog **in the yard** was barking.
>
> The preposition "in" connects the phrase "in the yard" to the noun "dog". Therefore it is an adjective phrase. The word "yard" would be the object of the preposition "in".

Exercise C

Underline the phrase in each of the following sentences. In the space provided after each sentence, write "ADJ" if it is an adjective phrase, and "ADV" if it is an adverb phrase.

1. The cars raced <u>in a circle</u>.   ADV
2. The clouds in the sky threatened rain. _____
3. The members of the team sat together. _____
4. The sign over the doorway was lit up. _____
5. The children sang in the choir. _____
6. The horses ran around the track. _____
7. Since yesterday he has been sleeping. _____
8. He cannot play for the school team. _____
9. She searched throughout the house for her jacket. _____
10. The students of grade four enjoy doing homework. _____
11. I have new friends since yesterday. _____

Exercise D

Complete each sentence with an adjective or adverb phrase.

The prepositions are italicized.

1. The boys went swimming *in* _____the river_____ .
2. We looked at the fish *in* _____ .
3. Place your boots *on* _____ .
4. The players *on* _____ celebrated the victory.
5. He arrived *at* _____ .
6. Do you like to play *in* _____ ?
7. The teachers *at* _____ are very strict.

A **Conjunction** connects words or groups of words.
Some familiar conjunctions are: **and**   **but**   **or**   **yet**   **nor**   **so**   **but**
Example: You **and** I are best friends.

Exercise E

Complete each of the following sentences by creating details to follow the conjunction. The conjunctions are italicized.

1. I called at your home *but* ____you were not there____ .
2. Pop *and* _____ make for a tasty treat.
3. It rained all night *but* _____ .
4. Either you come to my house *or* _____ .
5. I will help you *if* _____ .
6. Either he is laughing *or* _____ .
7. We will go to the beach *and* _____ .
8. Snow *and* _____ make for poor driving conditions.
9. We will go on holiday, come rain *or* _____ .

A **Subordinating Conjunction** joins an independent clause (a sentence) with a dependent clause. A dependent clause needs additional information for it to be complete.

Example: **While** I was walking to school, I found some money.

"I found some money" is an independent clause (complete sentence).

"While I was walking to school" is a dependent clause because it is incomplete on its own.

Exercise 7

Combine each pair of clauses by using the subordinating conjunction in parentheses ( ).

1. You can show me a better way / I will do it my own way   (unless)

   _____

2. She was the oldest / she made all the rules   (because)

   _____

3. We played the entire game / we were very tired   (even though)

   _____

4. You are sure this is the right way to go / we will follow you   (if)

   _____

5. I was talking on the phone / Sophia was watching a cartoon   (while)

   _____

CHALLENGE

There is a word missing in each of the incorrect sentences below. Can you figure out what is missing and add the word needed? Place your word in the space provided.

1. Baseball a great summer game.   _____

2. I caught a fish I was sleeping in the boat.   _____

3. A needle in a haystack is hard find.   _____

9 Building Complex Sentences

An **Independent Clause** is a group of words containing a subject and a verb that expresses a complete idea. Another name for the independent clause is the **Simple Sentence**.

The **Dependent Clause** is often referred to as a **Subordinate Clause**. It is dependent because, although it has a subject and a verb, it needs more information to make it complete. A dependent clause cannot stand alone; it needs the help of an independent clause (simple sentence).

Exercise A

Decide which kind of clause each group of words represents, and write the type of clause in the space provided.

There are 6 dependent clauses below.

1. Before the game started. _____
2. Whenever we go to our cottage. _____
3. It rained the entire time. _____
4. Instead of playing basketball. _____
5. My friends and I like to ride bikes. _____
6. Her dog chases cars, but always comes when called. _____
7. In the early morning sunlight. _____
8. The school emptied when the fire alarm sounded. _____
9. While we were waiting for the bus. _____
10. Since you asked for my help. _____

Exercise B

Underline the independent clause in each of the complex sentences below.

1. Whenever we go to the movies, we buy popcorn.
2. She told us to wait until we all finished our homework.

3. If the weather is clear, we can have a barbecue.
4. After we watch our favourite television show, we go right to bed.
5. Once the bell rings, recess is over.
6. He is happy now that his bike is fixed.
7. As long as we live close by, we can walk to school.
8. The students practised running when it was track and field season.
9. Because she was late for class, she had to go to the office first.
10. My father was looking forward to the holidays because he could take time off work.

Complex Sentences

When a dependent clause is joined to an independent clause by a subordinating conjunction, a complex sentence is formed.

Some of the most frequently used subordinating conjunctions are: **because, although, unless, whenever, after, as, as if, before, wherever, until**...

Exercise C

Make a complex sentence by putting a dependent clause in the space following the subordinating conjunction in each of the sentences below.

Make sure the clause has a "subject" and a "verb". Do not construct phrases.

1. If _____ , I will gladly help you.
2. He said he would meet me *when* _____ .
3. I will do *whatever* _____ .
4. She invited me to her house *after* _____ .
5. If _____ , we will celebrate.
6. Until _____ , I had never been to a circus.
7. We went on holiday *when* _____ .
8. The teacher asked us to finish our work *before* _____ .
9. Meet me in the school yard *when* _____ .
10. I asked my friend to tell me *where* _____ .

CHALLENGE

Combine the following choppy sentences into longer sentences.

You might have to change the order of the clauses or begin the sentence with the subordinating conjunction.

Example:

I enjoy eating candy. I go to the movies. (when)
When I go to the movies, I enjoy eating candy.   or
I enjoy eating candy when I go to the movies.

1. We went back to school. It was Monday. (because)

2. The school play was cancelled. Most of the participants were taken ill. (when)

3. The rain ended. The sun came out. (after)

4. We waited for hours. The bus finally came. (until)

5. The postman brought the mail. It was nearly noon hour. (when)

6. We began to do our work. The morning announcements were made. (after)

7. We get very tired. We have basketball practice. (whenever)

8. We are allowed. We will go to the game after school. (if)

Using Verbals

In an earlier unit, we learnt a verb form called gerund which ends in "ing". Gerunds are verbals that are used as nouns in a sentence.

Example (1): **Running** is a vigorous activity.

In this example, the **subject** of the sentence is "running" which is a verbal.

Example (2): He enjoys **running** with his team-mates.

In this case, "running" is an **object**. It is what he enjoys doing. "He" is the subject of the sentence, and "running" is the object.

Exercise D

Underline the gerund in each sentence below and state in the space whether it is the subject or the object.

1. Skiing can be dangerous. _____

2. We like biking along the mountain trails. _____

3. There is nothing better than eating ice cream on a hot day. _____

4. We all picked swimming as our favourite cottage activity. _____

Verbals instead of Dependent Clauses

A verbal can replace a long dependent clause and make the sentence easier to read.

Example: **While he was running** for the bus, he tripped and fell.   becomes
Running for the bus, he tripped and fell.

Exercise E

Finish each sentence below by replacing the dependent clause with a verbal.

1. When he was skiing down the hill, he fell.

   He fell _____.

2. When she was playing with the toys, she was happy.

   _____, she was happy.

3. While he was listening to music, he started to dance.

   _____, he started to dance.

10 Relative Clauses

The Restrictive Relative Clause

A restrictive clause (also called defining clause) gives necessary information to the sentence, particularly in defining or modifying a noun or verb.

Example: The boy arrived at school today. (no clause)

The boy who was new to the school arrived at school today. (restrictive clause)

The clause "who was new to the school" adds important information to describe the noun, boy.

Note that the restrictive clause is not separated from the rest of the sentence by commas.

Relative pronouns are used to introduce relative clauses. The common relative pronouns are: who, what, whom, whose, which, that, where, when, why.

Exercise A

Underline the restrictive relative clause in each of the sentences below.

1. The teachers who were located on the lower floor complained of cold classrooms.
2. The park where we used to play hide-and-seek is no longer there.
3. Textbooks that are no longer used were sent to needy countries.
4. Animals that are facing extinction must be protected.
5. The parents whose children took the school bus were asked to register.
6. The teacher rewarded the person who scored the highest results in the test.

Exercise B

Add your own restrictive relative clauses to make the sentences below more interesting.

1. The game was finally played.
   The game that was delayed by rain was finally played.

2. The children went for a cool dip in the swimming pool.
   _____

3. Her house was difficult to find.
   _____

4. The dog barked loudly.
   _____

5. The house was hard to get to.
   _____

6. The hockey team was unbeatable.
   _____

7. People crowded outside the ticket office.
   _____

Exercise C

Complete the following sentences that have restrictive relative clauses.

1. The words that were spoken by the student _____
2. The barn which was home to the cows _____
3. Birds that fly south for the winter _____
4. She wanted a car that was reliable _____
5. The bus that picks us up every morning _____
6. The student whose painting is displayed in the hallway _____

Exercise D

Finish the sentences by completing the restrictive relative clauses.

1. The dog that _____ is fun to play with.
2. The dog belongs to the boy who _____ .
3. The tree which _____ is fun to climb.
4. He was laughing at the clown who _____ .
5. They bought the house that _____ .
6. The player whom _____ is my brother.

The Non-Restrictive Relative Clause (also called non-defining clause) gives information that is not necessary to the basic meaning of the sentence. This information often adds interest to the sentence. Note that a non-restrictive relative clause is set off, before and after, by commas.

Example: The house, which had yellow shutters, was their home for many years.

The non-restrictive clause "which had yellow shutters" is not essential to the understanding of the sentence. It simply adds additional information.

Exercise E

Underline the non-restrictive clauses in the following sentences and add commas.

1. The dog which had a fluffy white coat played in the park.
2. His friend who was very reliable joined in the games they were playing.
3. The student who wore a green coat stood in the cold waiting for the school bus.
4. Relatives many of whom I didn't recognize arrived from everywhere.
5. Her friend who lives on the same street went away for the holidays.
6. Discussions about the environment which we enjoy are usually interesting.
7. The vacation which came in March gave us a much needed break from school.
8. Students who were carrying their knapsacks hurried into the school.
9. The boy who was riding a bicycle stopped at the store to make a purchase.

Exercise F

Complete the non-restrictive relative clause in each sentence below.

1. The skater, who _____ , won the competition.
2. The idea, which _____ , was the solution to the problem.
3. His friend, who _____ , was a great addition to the team.
4. The letter, which _____ , contained the information.

5. My uniform, which _____, was one size too big.
6. Sandy, whose _____, also sings and dances well.

Exercise G

Add non-restrictive clauses to the following sentences to make them more interesting.

The bold words in the sentences below suggest where you might add your non-restrictive relative clauses.

1. The **girl** won the **race**.
   The girl, who wore the blue top, won the race.

2. The **people** assembled in front of the **court house**.
   _____

3. **Hot dogs** were served in the **park**.
   _____

4. His **hat** was found in the **schoolyard**.
   _____

5. My **uncle** took me to the **cottage**.
   _____

6. Before the **boy** spoke out in class, everything was quiet.
   _____

7. The **passengers** grew impatient waiting for the **next train**.
   _____

8. The **actors** took to the **stage**.
   _____

9. The **animals** looked hungry.
   _____

10. He bought a **coat** from the **sports store**.
    _____

11 Developing the Paragraph

A **Paragraph** is a group of sentences that expresses a common idea. It is made up of the following:

Topic sentence – introduces main idea
Body sentences – develop the main idea by adding information in logical order
Conclusion – summarizes topic; adds further thought; links to next paragraph

Exercise A

For each paragraph, choose the most appropriate topic sentence and write it in the space provided. Give a title to the paragraph as well.

Paragraph 1

Topic sentences:
- Puppies love to chase a ball.
- Lauren's birthday present was a fluffy, little pup.
- Dogs make good companions.

Title: _____

_____ . She got this puppy when it was only eight weeks old and named it Abbey. Abbey loves to chase a tennis ball around the yard. At night the puppy curls up on her bed and goes to sleep. Lauren has promised her parents that she will take very good care of her new puppy.

Paragraph 2

Topic sentences:
- Canada is a very large country.
- This summer, we will travel across Canada.
- Driving long distances can be tiring.

Title: _____

_____ . My father showed us the route we will take across Canada. It will take us seven days to reach

Vancouver from our home in Toronto. We will drive through five provinces including Ontario and British Columbia. We are excited because we have never travelled outside Ontario.

Paragraph 3

Topic sentences:

- With two out in the ninth inning, we were losing by one run.
- A close score in baseball makes for an exciting finish.
- Sometimes a baseball game goes into extra innings.

Title: _____

_____ . Randall was our last chance to tie the game. He was very nervous. With two strikes on him, he took one final swing at the ball and connected for a home run. At that point we evened the score, but we went on to lose in the first extra inning. Although our glory didn't last long, we had fun playing in such an exciting game.

Paragraph 4

Topic sentences:

- Birthdays are often celebrated by eating cake.
- Kara had kept her birthday a secret from everyone at school except her best friend.
- Lisa is Kara's best friend.

Title: _____

_____ . When everyone in the class stood up and sang "Happy Birthday To You", Kara was shocked and embarrassed. She had not told anyone about her birthday. Her friend, Lisa, brought a huge cake and everyone in the class had a slice. Once the shock wore off, Kara enjoyed the rest of her special day.

Organizing Sentences into a Paragraph

A paragraph begins with a topic sentence which introduces the main idea of the paragraph. The body of the paragraph is made up of sentences that give information about the main idea. They should be arranged in a logical order to best develop the main idea of the paragraph. Often, these sentences will appear in the order that events happen.

Exercise B

Arrange each group of sentences below into a well-organized paragraph. Write the letters in the spaces provided.

1. A. Raking these leaves can be tiring.
   B. Bags and bags of leaves will be filled before the winter arrives.
   C. If the leaves aren't raked, there will be a mess in the yard when the spring arrives.
   D. The fall is here and the leaves will fill our backyards.

   | 1 | 2 | 3 | 4 |

2. A. I have just started to read the *Lord of the Rings* series of books.
   B. *Harry Potter* and *Lord of the Rings* are two of the most popular children's books.
   C. Many of my classmates have read all the books in both series.
   D. When I have finished that series, I will begin to read the *Harry Potter* series.

   | 1 | 2 | 3 | 4 |

3. A. The lake water was cooler than expected.
   B. It was a hot summer day and we were anxious to cool off.
   C. We decided to take a dip on the lake nearby.
   D. However, we soon got used to the chilly water and felt refreshed.

   | 1 | 2 | 3 | 4 |

Exercise C

For each topic sentence below, write a short paragraph of four sentences.

> Make sure that your sentences give information about the main idea stated in the topic sentence. The last sentence should be a concluding thought.

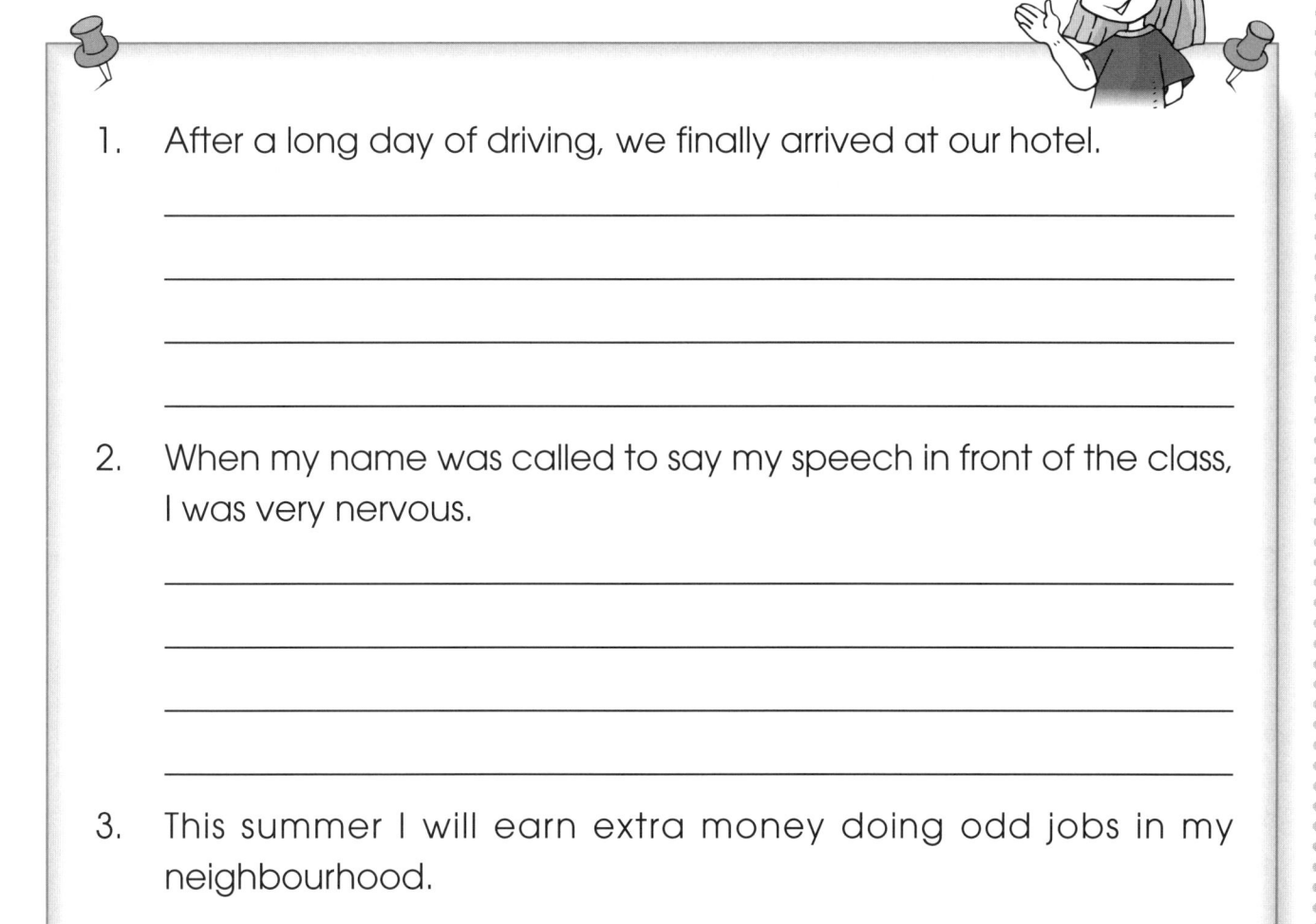

1. After a long day of driving, we finally arrived at our hotel.

2. When my name was called to say my speech in front of the class, I was very nervous.

3. This summer I will earn extra money doing odd jobs in my neighbourhood.

4. My friends and I decided to put on a show at school for Parents' Night.

EnglishSmart – Grammar · Grade 4

12 Rules of Punctuation

Punctuation Marks are symbols to help the reader better understand what is being written. They tell a reader when to pause, when a sentence ends, and when a sentence should be read with emphasis.

End Punctuation
1. A declarative sentence makes a simple statement of fact or information. It ends with a period (.).
2. An interrogative sentence asks a question. It ends with a question mark (?).
3. An imperative sentence gives an order. It ends with a period (.).
4. An exclamatory sentence shows emotion. It ends with an exclamation mark (!).

Exercise A

Of the six sentences below, four have incorrect end punctuation. Circle the number of the incorrectly punctuated sentences and make the necessary corrections.

1. Look out.
2. I wondered why they hadn't arrived yet?
3. What time did her party begin?
4. I would like all the grade four students to sit over here.
5. Never swim without supervision?
6. Ouch, that hurts.

Be careful of sentences that seem to be emphatic but are really just simple statements.

End punctuation such as the period has other grammatical uses. Periods are also the end punctuation for most abbreviations.

Exercise B

Write the abbreviation form of each of the following words and include the proper punctuation.

1. mister   _____
2. United States   _____
3. miss   _____
4. in the afternoon _____
5. doctor   _____
6. in the morning _____
7. British Columbia _____
8. Prince Edward Island _____
9. Newfoundland   _____
10. company (i.e. business) _____

The **Comma** is one of the most frequently used punctuation marks. Some of the uses of a comma are:

1. To create a mild pause in a sentence – If you don't hurry, you will be late.
2. To separate items in a list – He likes to play baseball, soccer, tennis, football, and basketball.
3. To set off a subordinate clause – While he waited for a bus, he read his book.
4. To introduce and follow a quotation – Ashley said, "Wait for me after school."
   "Wait for me after school," said Ashley.
5. To set off introductory words and phrases – Well, you finally arrived.
6. To set off descriptions in apposition – My teacher, Miss Johnson, is new to our school.

Exercise C

There are many commas missing in the following paragraph. Place commas where you think they belong according to the rules above.

There are 24 missing commas.

The Championship Game

Monday after school we played basketball for the city championship. Our coach Mr. Phillips said "I want everyone to try their hardest today." When the referee threw up the jump ball the game had started. They missed their first shot and we took the ball the length of the court for our first score. We knew that if we didn't play defence we would lose. Each of us covered our man and we allowed them to score very few baskets. The spectators cheered screamed clapped and waved their arms during the game. Oddly enough the opposition managed to even the score in the last minute of play. The championship came down to the last play of the game and we had the ball.

Slowly carefully and with great care we brought the ball up the floor. Jamie our team captain called a time-out. We huddled around our coach and he said "Make sure the last shot is a good one." Jamie on a pass from Rick dribbled to the corner spun around and threw up a rather long shot. The coach was not happy when this happened. But much to our surprise the next sound we heard was "Swish".

The Apostrophe

The following are some common rules of **apostrophe** use:

1. Use an apostrophe to show possession.

Examples: We did this **week's** math quiz on Tuesday.
We ordered our food from the **children's** menu.
The **teachers'** staff room is upstairs.

2. Use an apostrophe in contractions.

Example: He **has not** got a chance to win the race.   becomes
He **hasn't** got a chance to win the race.

3. Use an apostrophe to show the plural of letters of the alphabet, abbreviations, dates, and numerals. Also, an apostrophe is needed to show numbers missing.

Examples: The children in kindergarten learned their **abc's**.
My grandfather was born in the **40's**.
The last time the Maple Leafs won the Stanley Cup was **'67**.

Exercise D

Add the missing apostrophes. Make any other changes that are necessary.

1. Form contractions

   a. was not _____   b. I will _____
   c. will not _____   d. he has _____
   e. did not _____   f. it is _____
   g. can not _____   h. is not _____
   i. I am _____   j. do not _____

2. Shorten numbers

   a. 1962 _____
   b. 2002 _____
   c. 1995 _____

3. Make plurals

   a. 1950s _____
   b. p and q _____
   c. 5 _____

4. Change nouns to possessive form

   a. Paul _____   b. team _____
   c. boy _____   d. women _____
   e. Ross _____   f. doctors _____

Quotation Marks are used to contain the exact words of a speaker. They are also used to indicate the titles of songs, plays, television programmes, newspaper and magazine articles, and other short works.

Quotation marks are used to indicate that certain words, phrases, or sentences belong to someone else or are taken out of a book.

Example: It is important to remember that "no man is an island" and therefore we should all work together.

The phrase "no man is an island" was taken from a poem by Jonne Donne, and therefore, must be recognized as an outside source by using quotations.

Exercise E

In the following sentences, add quotations where necessary and any other punctuation that is needed.

1. When are you going on holiday asked my friend, Lucy.

2. We watched Malcolm in the Middle last night on television.

3. Linda said I'll be home late tonight.

4. The teacher read an article from a magazine entitled Getting Better Marks in School.

5. My family went to see The Lion King and heard the cast sing The Lion Sleeps Tonight.

6. My father always sings his favourite song, All You Need Is Love.

7. Do you want to put on a skit in front of the class asked Antoinetta.

8. It could be titled A Day in the Life of a Grade Four Student as she suggested.

9. The Man with Two Faces is one of Joanna's favourite chapters in the Harry Potter book, *Harry Potter and the Philosopher's Stone*.

10. Lauren and Dayna sang Happy Birthday to You to their friend, Victoria, at her surprise birthday party.

13 Punctuation, Capitalization, and Abbreviations

The Semicolon
Two related independent clauses are often joined by a conjunction. They can also be joined by a semicolon if they are related in topic.

Example: The weather was awful; it rained all night long.
Notice that the topic is bad weather, and the clause following the semicolon adds information or supports the idea of the clause that goes before it.

Exercise A

Match each independent clause from Column A with a related one from Column B. Write the independent clauses connected by a semicolon in the spaces provided.

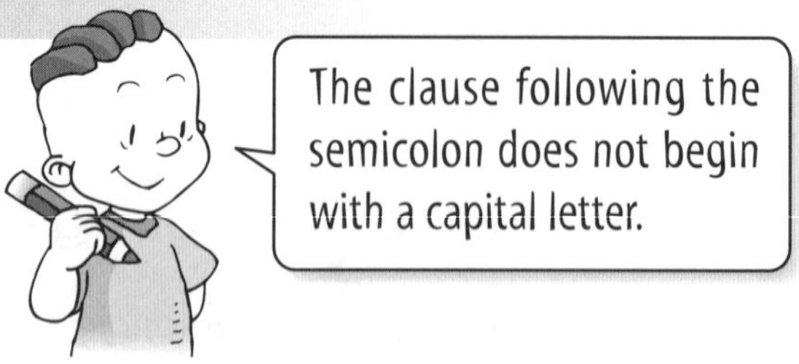

The clause following the semicolon does not begin with a capital letter.

Column A

1. The final minute of the game was exciting.
2. Paul was an excellent artist.
3. Rain poured down for most of the morning.
4. The fire alarm sounded.
5. His new bicycle was stolen.
6. The science test was scheduled for Friday.

Column B

- The ground was too soggy for a soccer game.
- The police said they would look for it.
- His paintings were hung in the hallway.
- Therefore, I studied for most of Thursday night.
- Luckily, it was only a drill.
- The score was tied.

1. _____
2. _____
3. _____
4. _____
5. _____
6. _____

The **Colon** is used to:

1. introduce a series of items.

Example: She likes to eat the following fruits: apples, peaches, pears, and plums.

2. set off a phrase that explains an idea that comes before.

Example: The school rule is as follows: students are expected to be on time.

3. set off an explanatory term (also known as an appositive).

Example: The school did fundraising for one reason only: to buy more reference books.

Exercise B

Insert a colon in the proper place in each sentence below.

1. Danny plays many sports basketball, tennis, soccer, and baseball.
2. The teacher has one request all pupils complete their homework.
3. He had a great idea to form a homework club.
4. You have to remember never play with matches again.
5. She invited the following friends Amanda, Olivia, Samantha, and Jessica.
6. Roger had one main goal he wanted to win the scoring title.
7. Her parents asked her to do the following empty the dishwasher, clean her room, and take out the garbage.
8. They brought their pets to school for one reason show-and-tell.

CHALLENGE

Place either a semicolon or a colon in the space provided in each sentence below.

If you are uncertain, review the examples above.

1. He ran his best race ___ yet, he did not win.
2. The referee tossed the coin ___ we got the ball first.
3. For our family trip, we packed the following ___ clothes, food, games, and books.
4. My mom says a holiday for her would include ___ reading a good book, relaxing by the lake, and sleeping in each morning.
5. A holiday for my dad has one meaning ___ no work.

Capitalization

1. Capitalize the first word in a sentence – **I**t was a beautiful day.
2. Capitalize proper nouns and adjectives including titles – **J**ohn was a **C**anadian who lived on **E**lm **S**treet. **H**e worked at the university and was called **P**rofessor **S**mith.
3. Capitalize specific places – We travelled to **B**anff, **A**lberta.
4. Capitalize days, weeks, months, holidays, and events – **R**emembrance **D**ay falls on **N**ovember 11; in the year 2001, it was on a **S**unday.
5. Capitalize the names of organizations – He played hockey in the **N**ational **H**ockey **L**eague. His father worked for the **M**unicipality, and was a member of the **R**otary **C**lub.
6. Capitalize races, nationalities, religions, and languages – My friend is a **C**atholic; he attends **S**t. **M**ary's **C**hurch. He speaks **S**panish, **E**nglish, and **F**rench.

Exercise C

With a dark pen or pencil, write over the letters that should be capitalized in each sentence. In the space following each sentence, put in the rule number that matches your correction.

1. my father doesn't get home until after supper some nights when he has to work late. _____
2. My friend and I joined the boy scouts. _____
3. My uncle works for the department of transport. _____
4. This summer, we will travel to quebec city. _____
5. Although she was french, she spoke german and italian. _____
6. We celebrate canada day each year on July 1. _____
7. The cities of montreal and quebec are on the st. lawrence river. _____
8. Every summer we go to the canadian national exhibition. _____

CHALLENGE

Circle the words in the following sentences that should not be capitalized.

There are four improper capitals.

1. The Atlantic Ocean is sometimes a very rough Ocean to cross. Many Ships have sunk in the enormous waves.
2. My cousin lives in the East, just North-east of the city of Halifax.
3. The Company my dad works for is the Ford Motor Company.

Abbreviations

In most cases it is a good idea to avoid abbreviations. However, they are acceptable in some situations.

Exercise D

Match each of the abbreviations below with the standard, expanded form of the word or phrase.

A. after noon B. mister C. doctor D. inches
E. miles F. before noon G. number
H. road I. United States of America J. versus
K. for example L. centimetres

1. no. _____
2. a.m. _____
3. in. _____
4. p.m. _____
5. Dr. _____
6. Mr. _____
7. Rd. _____
8. e.g. _____
9. mi. _____
10. U.S.A. _____
11. vs. _____
12. cm. _____

CHALLENGE

Here are some common abbreviations. Can you write the standard, expanded form of each abbreviation?

1. RCMP _____
2. Mt. _____
3. Jr. _____
4. Ave. _____
5. TV _____

Do the Challenge above ASAP. Do you know what ASAP is short for?

Answer: 6. _____

14 Tips for Effective Writing

Complete Sentences

Always double check your sentences to make sure that they contain a subject and a verb.

Example: Incorrect – Sharon looking out the window.
This sentence lacks a verb. The word "looking" is a verbal.
Correct – Sharon **was looking** out the window.

Exercise A

For each of the following sentences, write S for subject or V for verb to indicate which is missing. Write the corrected sentence in the space provided.

One of the sentences below is missing both a subject and verb.

1. The store owner up the shop early. _____

2. Paul across the field to get the ball. _____

3. Looked everywhere for my missing cat. _____

4. She down the street in the rain. _____

5. To earn extra money to buy a new bike. _____

Subject–Verb Agreement

In properly written sentences the subject and verb must agree in number and in person.

Example: Incorrect – There's lots of coins in the jar.

It should be: "There are lots of coins in the jar."

Exercise B

Cross out the incorrect verb in each of the following sentences and write the correct one in the space provided.

1. Paul and Richard was best friends. _____

2. The group are arriving this afternoon. _____
3. He always want me to show him my work. _____
4. Bacon and eggs is his favourite meal. _____
5. Anita and Rachel plays computer games. _____
6. The teacher walk up and down when he teaches a lesson. _____
7. The ballerina dance with strength and grace. _____
8. John accidentally thrown the ball through the window. _____

Short, Choppy Sentences

Short sentences are effective if they express an emotion. Too many short sentences, particularly when they are repetitive, can be annoying to the reader.

Example (1): Look out, there's a car coming!
(This sentence is effective because it is emphatic.)

Example (2): We played baseball. We played all afternoon.
(These two sentences should be combined to become "We played baseball all afternoon.")

Exercise C

Try not to leave out any details. Remove repeated words.

Combine the following choppy sentences to form one sentence.

1. It was the morning. It was raining. It was raining hard.

_____

2. The game began. The game began on time. The game began in the afternoon.

_____

3. We had pizza. The pizza was for our lunch. The pizza was delicious. The pizza was free.

_____

4. We stood in a line-up. The line-up was to see the first *Harry Potter* movie.

_____

5. We ran. We jumped. We skipped. We went across the schoolyard.

_____

Common Punctuation Errors

Here are a few common punctuation errors:

1. **Apostrophe Use**:
   a. Possessive Form: Incorrect: He borrowed Pauls bicycle.
                         Correct: He borrowed Paul's bicycle.
   b. Contractions: Incorrect: We cant go out this afternoon.
                         Correct: We can't go out this afternoon.

2. **Comma Use**:
   a. With items in a list: Incorrect: He wears a hat a scarf and gloves in winter.
                              Correct :   He wears a hat, a scarf, and gloves in winter.
   b. With subordinate clauses: Incorrect: We arrived, after the game was over.
                                  Correct: We arrived after the game was over.
   But, if the subordinate clause comes first in the sentence, follow it with a comma.
   Example: After the game was over, we arrived.
   c. To introduce a quotation: Incorrect: My mother asked "What time are you coming home?"
                                  Correct: My mother asked, "What time are you coming home?"
   d. Commas with dates: Incorrect: The party was scheduled for Tuesday August 6 2002.
                           Correct: The party was scheduled for Tuesday, August 6, 2002.

Exercise D

Find and correct the apostrophe and comma errors in the sentences below. Write the corrected sentences.

1. My friend said "The movie begins at two oclock."

2. We brought cookies cakes buns and pies to the bake sale.

3. I dont like trying to do things that I cant do.

4. She doesn't like waiting in line at the show to buy popcorn candy pop and ice cream.

5. Whenever we go shopping we always spend too much money.

6. I will be able to stay over at your house, if I finish cleaning my room.

Confusing Homonyms

Homonyms are words that sound the same but are spelled differently.

Examples: whole/hole, have/half, buy/by, here/hear, write/right, scene/seen, brake/break

Exercise E

In each sentence below there is a pair of homonyms to choose from. Read the sentence carefully to get its meaning, and circle the correct homonym.

1. It's / Its Jason who broke the vase.
2. We lost hour / our weigh/way in the fog.
3. Do you no / know which / witch way to go to the fare/fair?
4. We had too / two much homework on the weekend.
5. The plane / plain landed on the plane / plain.
6. If you drink the dye / die, you could die / dye.
7. My dad slammed on the car break / brake to avoid hitting the bear / bare on the highway.
8. Whose / Who's book is this?

Double Negatives

Try to avoid using more than one negative word in a sentence. Some examples of negative words are: don't, wasn't, none, no, never, no more, no one.

Some positive replacement words are: any, anyone, ever.

Example: Incorrect: He doesn't give no help to no one.

It should be: "He doesn't give any help to anyone."

Exercise F

In the sentences below, the negative words are underlined. Cross out the unnecessary negatives and change them to positive words.

1. Sheila <u>wasn't</u> <u>never</u> going to go there again.
2. Phillip <u>hasn't</u> got <u>no</u> choice but to take the school bus home.
3. He <u>didn't</u> give us <u>none</u> of the information for our project.
4. They <u>didn't</u> ask <u>nobody</u> if they <u>weren't</u> coming to the party.
5. She <u>didn't</u> tell <u>no one</u> the answer.

15 Writing Descriptive and Narrative Paragraphs

Descriptive Paragraphs
The purpose of a descriptive paragraph is to describe an action, an event, or a place. The use of vivid adjectives and adverbs will help to bring your descriptive passage to life for the reader.

Sensory Details
Sensory details appeal to our sense of smell, taste, touch, and hearing.

Exercise A

Fill in the sensory detail chart below with types of sights, sounds, and textures (things that you can feel) that might be common to the places in the chart. Try to include at least <u>two details</u> for each place in the chart.

At the amusement park, you might hear bells ringing as the rides start up.

Senses	Amusement Park	Restaurant	The Beach
Sight	1. 2. 3.	1. 2. 3.	1. 2. 3.
Sound	1. 2. 3.	1. 2. 3.	1. 2. 3.
Touch	1. 2. 3.	1. 2. 3.	1. 2. 3.

Writing Descriptive and Narrative Paragraphs

In Exercise A, you listed sensory details for each of the three places. Next, for each of those details, write a descriptive word.

Example: If you were describing the bells whistling at an amusement park, you could use various adjectives, such as: **loud** bells, **soft** bells, **clanging** bells.

You could compare the bells to other kinds of bells that your reader might be familiar with such as: church bells, cow bells, school bells, or fire engine bells.

You might use the word **like** to explain the type of bell ringing sound that you want to describe.

Example: When the rides were ready to go, a ring **like a church bell** rang loudly.

Exercise B

Choose one of the topics (amusement park, beach, restaurant) from the chart in Exercise A. In the chart below, list the details from that topic. Place a descriptive word (adjective, adverb, or comparison) beside each of the details in the space provided. This will also be the topic of your paragraph writing in Exercise C.

Title: _____

Detail from your list	Description of the detail
Sight	**Sight**
1. _____	1. _____
2. _____	2. _____
3. _____	3. _____
Sound	**Sound**
1. _____	1. _____
2. _____	2. _____
3. _____	3. _____
Touch	**Touch**
1. _____	1. _____
2. _____	2. _____
3. _____	3. _____

Exercise C

Write a descriptive paragraph using one of the topics from Exercise A. Refer to the details and the descriptions listed in Exercise B.

Use the plan outlined below to construct your paragraph.

Title: Use one of the titles from Exercise A or create your own.

Topic Sentence: Introduces the main idea of your paragraph; gives the reader necessary details (who, what, where, when) about your topic; leads into your descriptive sentences.

Detail Sentences: In sentence form, describe the details that you have listed in Exercise B.

Concluding Sentence: Complete your paragraph with an idea that summarizes the ideas described or the topic in general.

Title: _____

Topic Sentence: _____
_____

First Detail: _____
_____

Second Detail: _____
_____

Third Detail: _____
_____

Concluding Idea: _____
_____

The **Narrative Paragraph** tells a story. It may use descriptive details like the descriptive paragraph, but its main purpose is the telling of a story. The story may be based on fact or may be fictitious, that is, based entirely on an imagined story. The story may be about a single event or a series of events.

Guidelines for Writing a Narrative Paragraph

1. Begin with a **topic sentence**. The topic sentence should give the reader information as to **where** or **when** your story takes place, **who** is involved in your story, and **what** your story is about.
2. When telling a story or relating an event, it is useful to place the events in the order in which they happened.
3. Use the following structure:

Beginning: Topic sentence

Middle: The sentences that give details of your story or events in the order in which they happen.

Ending (conclusion): The final sentence that offers an additional thought, a summary of the events, or something further for the reader to consider.

Exercise D

Write your narrative paragraph in the space below. You may choose from one of the following topics or create your own.

1. An Embarrassing Moment
2. Danger Was All Around Me
3. The Summer Adventure
4. The Worst Storm of the Winter

Title: _____

Progress Test 2

Prepositions and Conjunctions

Exercise A

Complete the sentences with suitable prepositions and conjunctions.

| under | with | and | of | in | over | for | or | but | until |

1. After the game, we went _____ an ice cream cone _____ the mall.
2. She found her lunch box in the classroom _____ the coats.
3. Lucy and Susie _____ the grade four class are best friends.
4. I think this is the answer _____ I'm not completely sure.
5. Shane must wait _____ tomorrow to get his new bikes.
6. Beside the phone is a phone book _____ a list of all my friends' numbers.
7. You either take the money _____ leave _____ you will lose all you have.
8. The poor dog was run _____ by a truck.

Adverb or Adjective Phrases

Only three of the phrases below are adjective phrases.

Exercise B

Identify whether each of the underlined phrases below are adjective or adverb phrases. Place "ADJ" or "ADV" in the space provided.

1. She placed her books <u>inside her school bag</u>. _____
2. The teachers <u>of our school</u> are very helpful. _____
3. <u>In the morning</u>, the paper is delivered <u>to our front door</u>. _____ _____
4. The runners raced <u>around the track</u>. _____
5. He played <u>for the local hockey team</u>. _____
6. The light <u>above the door</u> had burned out. _____
7. The boy <u>with the baseball glove</u> will pitch in the game. _____
8. I can't reach the box <u>on the top shelf</u>. _____

68 EnglishSmart – Grammar • Grade 4

Dependent and Independent Clauses

Exercise C

Complete each of the following sentences with an independent (main) clause.

1. Unless the school bus comes now, _____ .

2. If we do not hurry, _____ .

3. Until we all work together, _____ .

4. Whenever we play hockey outdoors, _____ .

5. Although she was late for school every day, _____
_____ .

Exercise D

Change one of the pairs of independent clauses into a dependent clause by introducing it with a subordinating conjunction.

> Use each subordinating conjunction only once. You may have to change the order of the phrases in the sentence.

| whenever | because | until |
| after | although | since |

1. we ate dinner / we watched television
   _____

2. I got a flat tire / I haven't been able to ride my bicycle
   _____

3. I slept in until noon / I was still tired
   _____

4. we have a picnic / it always rains
   _____

5. We couldn't go to the park / we didn't have a ride
   _____

6. We waited all day long / the bus arrived
   _____

Progress Test 2

Complex and Compound Sentences

A complex sentence is made up of an independent clause and at least one dependent clause. A compound sentence is made up of two independent clauses joined by a conjunction.

Exercise E

Read the following sentences. Write "complex" for complex sentences and "compound" for compound sentences.

1. While we waited for our cousins, we played Monopoly. _____
2. The game began and we took our seats. _____
3. Although the students practised for the play, they forgot their lines. _____
4. We won the game because we had the better team. _____
5. We will travel to the west coast or we will fly overseas. _____
6. Our teacher gives lots of homework but we like doing it. _____
7. They didn't say a word and continued to move on. _____

Verbals

Exercise F

Underline the gerund in each of the sentences below. Indicate whether each gerund is a subject or an object by writing "subject" or "object" in the space provided.

1. Running is good exercise. _____
2. She likes dancing to her favourite music. _____
3. The teacher enjoys writing on the blackboard. _____
4. Laughing is good for your health. _____
5. Swimming in that lake is prohibited. _____
6. Playing video games can be addictive. _____
7. Although skiing is an expensive sport, it is worth the cost. _____

Punctuation

Exercise G

Place the letter for the punctuation mark in the space that matches its rule of use.

Rule		Punctuation Mark
1. end of a sentence	___	A. an apostrophe
2. before and after a speech	___	B. commas
3. joins two independent clauses	___	C. a period
4. after an emphatic expression	___	D. a colon
5. follows an interrogative sentence	___	E. an exclamation mark
6. separates items in a list	___	F. a semicolon
7. comes before listing items	___	G. quotation marks
8. indicates possession	___	H. a question mark

Exercise H

In each sentence below, there are quotation marks missing. Add the necessary quotation marks and commas.

1. The grade four class memorized the poem The Vagabond Song by Bliss Carmen.

2. Scooby Doo is a very popular children's television show.

3. Shakespeare wrote the famous play Romeo and Juliet.

4. His father said Do not forget to take your house key with you.

5. What time will the movie end? she asked.

6. Gulliver's Travels is one of my favourite stories.

7. Think carefully before you make the decision the teacher reminded her.

8. One critic stated that the first Harry Potter book was a terrific read and a stunning first novel.

Progress Test 2

Exercise I

Place a semicolon or a colon in the blank space in each sentence below.

1. The morning sun melted the dew drops ___ the flowers were awakened.
2. To prepare for our trip, we purchased ___ maps, a cooler, a knapsack, and a flashlight.
3. The main idea of the story was basically ___ never be careless.
4. Sarah was the best artist in the school ___ that is, her art was always on display.
5. She couldn't go on anymore ___ she was too tired.
6. These students have to stay behind ___ Janet, Zoe, Fred, and Gord.

Exercise J

Re-write the following paragraph and add in the missing punctuation marks. Capitalize the words where necessary.

on canada day we went to ottawa for the celebration there were lots of people outside the parliament buildings although we were not able to get to the front we could get a good view of the stage the performance was superb and everyone had a good time do you want to stay for the firework display my father asked us of course we all responded excitedly

Relative Clauses

Exercise K

Underline the relative clause in each sentence below and put "R" (restrictive) or "NR" (non-restrictive) in the space provided.

1. Her birthday, which happened to fall on February 29, was reason to celebrate. _____
2. He required the information that was needed to do the job. _____
3. The winner who was exhausted from the race stumbled forward. _____
4. The teacher, who has been on staff for many years, organized a school play. _____
5. The dog, whose name was Scamp, was a very good watchdog. _____
6. The cake, which I gave Sam for his birthday, was made by my sister. _____
7. John's father, whom everyone likes, will be our coach. _____
8. I like teachers who care. _____

Exercise L

For each pair of sentences, change one into a relative clause to form a complex sentence.

1. The room was small but tidy. We would stay there for the night.
   _____

2. I like the backpack. My mom bought it for my tenth birthday.
   _____

3. The game was boring. It lasted more than four hours.
   _____

4. The boy was funny. We called him The Joker.
   _____

5. The tall structure is the CN Tower. It stands next to the SkyDome.
   _____

Grade 4 Answers

1 Nouns

A. 1. jumps 2. bulky 3. sings
   4. exciting 5. useful 6. happy
B. 1. Harry Potter 2. Joe Sakic
   3. CN Tower 4. Royal Bank
   5. Air Canada Centre 6. Wonderland
C. 1. <u>Ramon Gonzales</u> and his <u>sister</u>, <u>Julia</u>, attend <u>Williamson Road Public School</u>.
   2. They enjoy playing <u>sports</u> at recess <u>time</u>.
   3. <u>Ramon</u> is a very good basketball <u>player</u> while <u>Julia</u> prefers to play <u>volleyball</u>.
   4. The Gonzales <u>family</u> moved to <u>Canada</u> from <u>Spain</u> three <u>years</u> ago and live in a downtown <u>neighbourhood</u>.
   5. <u>Julia</u> and <u>Ramon</u> speak both <u>Spanish</u> and <u>English</u> and are learning <u>French</u> in <u>school</u>.
   6. <u>Mr. Gonzales</u> works as a computer <u>programmer</u> and <u>Mrs. Gonzales</u> is an interior <u>decorator</u>.
   7. In the Gonzales <u>family</u> there are four <u>children</u>, but only <u>two</u> of the <u>children</u> attend <u>school</u>.
   8. Next <u>summer</u>, the <u>family</u> will visit their <u>cousins</u> in <u>Spain</u>.
D. 1. armies – 4a 2. lunches – 3
   3. pens – 1 4. duties – 4a
   5. proofs – 2 6. ladies – 4a
   7. lives – 2 8. journeys – 4b
   9. halves – 2 10. patios – 5a
   11. taxes – 3 12. radios – 5a
   13. cars – 1 14. diaries – 4a
   15. churches – 3 16. leaves – 2

Challenge
1. These nouns are both singular and plural.
2. A. oxen B. mice
   C. children D. teeth
E. A. crew B. team C. gang
   D. army E. navy
   1. nation 2. company 3. crowd

2 Pronouns

A. 1. it 2. their 3. her 4. us
   5. their 6. us 7. it 8. We
   9. me 10. hers
B. 1. them 2. us 3. whom 4. her
   5. him 6. me 7. her
C. 1. her 2. his 3. their 4. our
   5. yours ; mine
D. 1. Which 2. Whose / What
   3. Who 4. Where
E. 1. It 2. They 3. their 4. Their
   5. them 6. him 7. them 8. they
   9. their 10. His 11. he 12. them
   13. their 14. They 15. them 16. they
   17. whom

Challenge
1. her – John tied his shoe.
2. ourselves – The boys kept the candy to themselves.
3. who – John wasn't sure to whom he should call.
4. our – The audience clapped their hands.
5. my – We took our time getting here.
a. themselves – We helped ourselves to the treats.
b. Whom – Who is at the door?
c. his – Cheryl hurt her foot.
d. our – I walked home on my own.
e. their – We raised our voices in the singing.

3 Adjectives

A. 1. tall ; his ; small
   2. cold ; tired
   3. deep ; older ; huge ; snow
   4. bright ; dark
   5. this ; adventure ; younger
   6. little ; short ; sweet
B. 1. small – smaller – smallest
   2. early – earlier – earliest
   3. happy – happier – happiest
   4. sad – sadder – saddest
   5. cheap – cheaper – cheapest
   6. fine – finer – finest
   7. kind – kinder – kindest
   8. new – newer – newest
C. 1. good – better – best 2. much – more – most
   3. bad – worse – worst 4. some – more – most
   5. little – less – least
D. 1. a 2. b 3. a 4. a
   5. a 6. b
E. 1. F 2. D 3. C 4. E
   5. G 6. H 7. A 8. B
F. (Suggested answers)
   1. hottest 2. wise 3. local
   4. bus 5. most 6. cool
   7. No Swimming 8. disappointed 9. public
   10. spacious

4 Adverbs

A. 2. loudly – how 3. always – when
   4. quickly – how 5. slowly – how
   6. soon – when 7. sincerely – how
   8. accurately – how ; quickly – how
   9. busily – how
   10. faster – how ; farther – where
   11. slightly – how
B. 1. entirely 2. greedily 3. fairly
   4. simply 5. sloppily 6. happily
   7. desperately 8. nicely 9. silently
   10. wearily
C. 1. <u>lazily</u> (along) 2. <u>sickly</u> (sweet)
   3. <u>incredibly</u> (early) 4. <u>entirely</u> (pleased)
   5. <u>desperately</u> (hungry) 6. <u>fairly</u> (dark)
   7. <u>badly</u> (injured) 8. <u>completely</u> (useless)
D. 1. He rides his bicycle more carefully than his brother.

Grade 4 Answers

2. He played hockey more skilfully than all his teammates.
3. The dogs in the cage barked more viciously than the dogs on leashes.
4. The librarian spoke more enthusiastically than our teacher about the book.
5. Her homework was more carefully done than mine.

E. 1. bad – worse – worst 2. well – better – best
3. badly – worse – worst

F. 1. excitedly 2. finally 3. vigorously
4. kindly 5. generously 6. wildly
7. dangerously 8. incredibly 9. easily

5 Verbs

A. 1. were playing 2. made
3. arrived ; phoned 4. rang ; began
5. ran ; sat ; watched

B. 1. The parents <u>applauded</u> the (performance) of the party.
2. He <u>shot</u> the (puck) into the net.
3. The girls in the class <u>sang</u> a (song) while the boys <u>performed</u> a (dance).
4. The bus driver <u>took</u> the passengers' (tickets) before leaving the depot.
5. The children <u>played</u> (baseball) in the schoolyard while the teachers <u>held</u> a (meeting).

C. 1. asked – T 2. ask – T 3. was – I
4. raced – I 5. played – T

D. 1. will 2. has 3. will
4. must 5. will

E. 2. catch – caught – catching – caught
3. cut – cut – cutting – cut
4. become – became – becoming – become
5. draw – drew – drawing – drawn
6. know – knew – knowing – known
7. hear – heard – hearing – heard
8. read – read – reading – read
9. wear – wore – wearing – worn
10. write – wrote – writing – written
11. go – went – going – gone
12. bite – bit – biting – bitten
13. sing – sang – singing – sung

F. 1. were ; organize 2. arrived
3. arrived ; had ; preparing
4. felt 5. trained
6. running 7. came ; placed
8. ran 9. taking ; waiting
10. finished

6 The Sentence

A. 1. <u>John</u> | <u>watched</u> a movie with his friends.
2. The tired <u>travellers</u> | <u>waited</u> at the bus terminal.
3. Most <u>swimmers</u> | <u>fear</u> the presence of sharks.
4. <u>Canada</u> | <u>is</u> the largest country in the world.
5. <u>He</u> | <u>will take</u> his bicycle with him on holiday.

6. <u>It</u> | <u>is</u> a beautiful day today.

B. (Suggested answers)
1. The horses and cows shared the barn.
2. She laughed and cried at the same time.
3. Red, blue, and yellow are her favourite colours.
4. He chewed, swallowed, and digested his food.
5. The girls and boys packed and carried the boxes.
6. Joanna or Maria will babysit tonight.
7. Janet washed and dried the clothes this morning.
8. I can see some hens and ducks over there.

C. 1. has 2. like 3. wants 4. are
5. were 6. play 7. are

D. (Answers may vary.)
1. School was cancelled so the students went home.
2. It was her birthday and she opened her presents.
3. The weather was awful but we played outside anyway.
4. We would be rewarded with treats if we did all our work.
5. The fishermen waited patiently but they didn't catch a thing.
6. They will be late if they miss the train.
7. The children played a vigorous game of soccer so they were all very tired.
8. The boys were hungry but there was nothing for them to eat.

E. (Answers will vary.)

7 Building Sentences with Descriptors

A. 1. French ; quietly 2. vicious ; fiercely
3. puffy ; lazily 4. hot ; mercilessly
5. young ; gracefully 6. reckless ; dangerously
7. brave ; fearlessly 8. best ; kindly

B. 1. in ; ADV 2. of ; ADJ 3. of ; ADJ
4. with ; ADJ 5. in ; ADJ 6. over ; ADV
7. of ; ADJ 8. from ; ADJ 9. at ; ADV
10. in ; ADV

C. 1. across the field ; over the hill
2. In the summertime ; by a small lake
3. in the textbook
4. At the beginning ; of our gym class
5. in front ; of the class
6. in the gymnasium
7. under our desks ; during the test
8. (no phrase) ; "when the rain came down" is a clause
9. in the house ; in the doghouse
10. in the clearing ; on the campfire

D. (Individual writing)

Challenge (Answers will vary.)

Progress Test 1

A. 1. sidewalk ; walker 2. sadness ; happiness
3. afternoon ; morning 4. children ; infant ; child
5. stranger

B. 1. Mount Everest
2. John

- C. 1. ox   2. mice   3. fishes / fish
  4. child   5. wives   6. lives
  7. teeth   8. foot
- D. 1. I – my / mine – we – our / ours
  2. she – her / hers – they – their / theirs
  3. it – its – they – their / theirs
  4. you – your / yours – you – your / yours
- E. 1. beautiful   2. weary
  3. careful ; careless   4. large ; big ; enormous
  5. golden   6. precious ; valuable
- F. 1. c   2. a   3. a   4. c
  5. a
- G. 1. happily   2. carelessly   3. quickly
  4. creatively   5. finally
- H. 1. chased ; picked   2. poured
  3. laughed ; wasn't   4. ate ; drank
  5. are
- I. 1. play – I
  2. chose – T ; would wear – I
  3. gave – T
  4. was speaking – I ; listened – I
  5. covered – T ; blew – I
- J. 1. were   2. had   3. could
  4. must   5. will
- K. 1. drew   2. saw   3. caught
  4. wrote   5. thought   6. read
  7. drove   8. had   9. did
  10. cried
- L. 1. The <u>team</u> | <u>played</u> football in the old stadium beside the river.
  2. Both the <u>boys</u> and the <u>girls</u> | <u>used</u> the same playing field during recess.
  3. The <u>audience</u> | <u>laughed</u> when they watched the funny movie.
  4. <u>We</u> | <u>wear</u> our gloves whenever it gets very cold.
  5. The tall <u>boys</u> | <u>played</u> basketball after school.
  6. <u>It</u> | <u>rains</u> whenever we plan a picnic.
- M. (Suggested answers)
  1. <u>Mike</u> and <u>Janet</u> <u>sang</u> and <u>laughed</u>.
  2. We ate <u>peanuts</u> and <u>popcorn</u> at the baseball game.
  3. We <u>laughed</u> and <u>cried</u> at the same time.
  4. They <u>created</u> and <u>presented</u> the project together.
  5. The children <u>jumped</u> and <u>splashed</u> in the water.
- N. 1. wants / wanted   2. enjoy ; enjoyed
  3. carry ; carried   4. go
  5. giggles ; is / giggled ; was
  6. drive ; drove   7. makes / made
  8. takes / took
- O. 1. of the house – ADJ ; in the morning – ADV
  2. Outside the window – ADV ; on a branch – ADV
  3. In the evening – ADV ; for a drive – ADV ; to town – ADJ

- 3. June ; July
- 4. Ottawa ; Ottawa River
- 5. Disneyland
- 6. The Toronto Maple Leafs ; NHL

- 4. in the parking lot – ADJ
- 5. of grade four – ADJ ; in the gymnasium – ADV
- 6. At the bottom – ADV ; of the pool – ADJ ; of the polo player – ADJ
- P. 1. Swimming – G
  2. Hiking in the mountains – VP
  3. Looking in store windows – VP ; spending money – VP
  4. Singing – G ; dancing – G
  5. walking in the rain – VP
  6. Skiing – G ; tobogganing down the hills – VP

8 Prepositions and Conjunctions

- A. 2. under   3. down   4. during
  5. across   6. of   7. between
  8. near   9. without   10. inside ; for
- B. (Individual writing)
- C. 2. in the sky – ADJ
  3. of the team – ADJ
  4. over the doorway – ADJ
  5. in the choir – ADV
  6. around the track – ADV
  7. Since yesterday – ADV
  8. for the school team – ADV
  9. throughout the house – ADV ; for her jacket – ADV
  10. of grade four – ADJ
  11. since yesterday – ADV
- D. (Answers will vary.)
- E. (Answers will vary.)
- F. (Suggested answers)
  1. Unless you can show me a better way, I will do it my own way.
  2. Because she was the oldest, she made all the rules.
  3. We played the entire game even though we were very tired.
  4. If you are sure this is the right way to go, we will follow you.
  5. While I was talking on the phone, Sophia was watching a cartoon.

Challenge (Suggested answers)
  1. Baseball is a great summer game.
  2. I caught a fish while I was sleeping in the boat.
  3. A needle in a haystack is hard to find.

9 Building Complex Sentences

- A. 1. dependent   2. dependent   3. independent
  4. dependent   5. independent   6. independent
  7. dependent   8. independent   9. dependent
  10. dependent
- B. 1. Whenever we go to the movies, <u>we buy popcorn</u>.
  2. <u>She told us to wait</u> until we all finished our homework.
  3. If the weather is clear, <u>we can have a barbecue</u>.
  4. After we watch our favourite television show, <u>we go right to bed</u>.
  5. Once the bell rings, <u>recess is over</u>.
  6. <u>He is happy</u> now that his bike is fixed.

7. As long as we live close by, <u>we can walk to school</u>.
8. <u>The students practised running</u> when it was track and field season.
9. Because she was late for class, <u>she had to go to the office first</u>.
10. <u>My father was looking forward to the holidays</u> because he could take time off work.

C. (Answers will vary.)

Challenge (Suggested answers)
1. We went back to school because it was Monday.
2. The school play was cancelled when most of the participants were taken ill.
3. After the rain ended, the sun came out.
4. We waited for hours until the bus finally came.
5. The postman brought the mail when it was nearly noon hour.
6. We began to do our work after the morning announcements were made.
7. We get very tired whenever we have basketball practice.
8. If we are allowed, we will go to the game after school.

D. 1. Skiing – subject 2. biking – object
   3. eating – object 4. swimming – object
E. 1. skiing down the hill 2. Playing with the toys
   3. Listening to music

10 Relative Clauses

A. 1. who were located on the lower floor
   2. where we used to play hide-and-seek
   3. that are no longer used
   4. that are facing extinction
   5. whose children took the school bus
   6. who scored the highest results in the test
B. (Individual writing)
C. (Individual writing)
D. (Individual writing)
E. 1. The dog, <u>which had a fluffy white coat</u>, played in the park.
   2. His friend, <u>who was very reliable</u>, joined in the games they were playing.
   3. The student, <u>who wore a green coat</u>, stood in the cold waiting for the school bus.
   4. Relatives, <u>many of whom I didn't recognize</u>, arrived from everywhere.
   5. Her friend, <u>who lives on the same street</u>, went away for the holidays.
   6. Discussions about the environment, <u>which we enjoy</u>, are usually interesting.
   7. The vacation, <u>which came in March</u>, gave us a much needed break from school.
   8. Students, <u>who were carrying their knapsacks</u>, hurried into the school.
   9. The boy, <u>who was riding a bicycle</u>, stopped at the store to make a purchase.
F. (Individual writing)

G. (Individual writing)

11 Developing the Paragraph

A. Titles (Answers will vary.)
   Topic sentences :
   1. Lauren's birthday present was a fluffy, little pup.
   2. This summer, we will travel across Canada.
   3. With two out in the ninth inning, we were losing by one run.
   4. Kara had kept her birthday a secret from everyone at school except her best friend.
B. 1. D ; C ; A ; B   2. B ; C ; A ; D
   3. B ; C ; A ; D
C. (Individual writing)

12 Rules of Punctuation

A. 1. Incorrect – Look out!
   2. Incorrect – I wondered why they hadn't arrived yet.
   3. Correct
   4. Correct
   5. Incorrect – Never swim without supervision.
   6. Incorrect – Ouch, that hurts!
B. 1. Mr.   2. US / U.S.   3. Ms.   4. p.m.
   5. Dr.   6. a.m.   7. B.C.   8. P.E.I.
   9. Nfld.   10. Co.
C.   Monday after school, we played basketball for the city championship. Our coach, Mr. Phillips, said, "I want everyone to try their hardest today." When the referee threw up the jump ball, the game had started. They missed their first shot, and we took the ball the length of the court for our first score. We knew that if we didn't play defence, we would lose. Each of us covered our man, and we allowed them to score very few baskets. The spectators cheered, screamed, clapped, and waved their arms during the game. Oddly enough, the opposition managed to even the score in the last minute of play. The championship came down to the last play of the game, and we had the ball.
   Slowly, carefully, and with great care, we brought the ball up the floor. Jamie, our team captain, called a time-out. We huddled around our coach and he said, "Make sure the last shot is a good one." Jamie, on a pass from Rick, dribbled to the corner, spun around, and threw up a rather long shot. The coach was not happy when this happened. But much to our surprise, the next sound we heard was "Swish".

D. 1. a. wasn't   b. I'll   c. won't
     d. he's   e. didn't   f. it's
     g. can't   h. isn't   i. I'm
     j. don't
   2. a. '62   b. '02   c. '95
   3. a. 1950's   b. p's and q's   c. 5's
   4. a. Paul's   b. team's   c. boy's
     d. women's   e. Ross's   f. doctors'

E. 1. "When are you going on holiday?" asked my friend, Lucy.
2. We watched "Malcolm in the Middle" last night on television.
3. Linda said, "I'll be home late tonight."
4. The teacher read an article from a magazine entitled "Getting Better Marks in School".
5. My family went to see "The Lion King" and heard the cast sing "The Lion Sleeps Tonight".
6. My father always sings his favourite song, "All You Need Is Love".
7. "Do you want to put on a skit in front of the class?" asked Antoinetta.
8. It could be titled "A Day in the Life of a Grade Four Student" as she suggested.
9. "The Man with Two Faces" is one of Joanna's favourite chapters in the Harry Potter book, *Harry Potter and the Philosopher's Stone*.
10. Lauren and Dayna sang "Happy Birthday to You" to their friend, Victoria, at her surprise birthday party.

13 Punctuation, Capitalization, and Abbreviations

A. 1. The final minute of the game was exciting; the score was tied.
2. Paul was an excellent artist; his paintings were hung in the hallway.
3. Rain poured down for most of the morning; the ground was too soggy for a soccer game.
4. The fire alarm sounded; luckily, it was only a drill.
5. His new bicycle was stolen; the police said they would look for it.
6. The science test was scheduled for Friday; therefore, I studied for most of Thursday night.

B. 1. Danny plays many sports: basketball, tennis, soccer, and baseball.
2. The teacher has one request: all pupils complete their homework.
3. He had a great idea: to form a homework club.
4. You have to remember: never play with matches again.
5. She invited the following friends: Amanda, Olivia, Samantha, and Jessica.
6. Roger had one main goal: he wanted to win the scoring title.
7. Her parents asked her to do the following: empty the dishwasher, clean her room, and take out the garbage.
8. They brought their pets to school for one reason: show-and-tell.

Challenge
1. ;   2. ;   3. :   4. :
5. :

C. 1. My – 1
2. Boy Scouts – 5
3. Department of Transport – 5
4. Quebec City – 3
5. French ; German ; Italian – 6
6. Canada Day – 4
7. Montreal ; Quebec ; St. Lawrence River – 3
8. Canadian National Exhibition – 2

Challenge
1. ocean ; ships   2. north-east   3. company

D. 1. G   2. F   3. D   4. A
5. C   6. B   7. H   8. K
9. E   10. I   11. J   12. L

Challenge
1. Royal Canadian Mounted Police
2. Mountain   3. Junior
4. Avenue   5. Television
6. as soon as possible

14 Tips for Effective Writing

A. (Suggested answers)
1. V – The store owner closed up the shop early.
2. V – Paul sprinted across the field to get the ball.
3. S – I looked everywhere for my missing cat.
4. V – She walked down the street in the rain.
5. S and V – He worked to earn extra money to buy a new bike.

B. 1. was – were / are
2. are – is
3. want – wants
4. is – are / were
5. plays – play / played
6. walk – walks
7. dance – dances / danced
8. thrown – threw

C. (Suggested answers)
1. It was raining hard in the morning.
2. The game began on time in the afternoon. / The afternoon game began on time.
3. We had free, delicious pizza for lunch.
4. We stood in a line-up to see the first *Harry Potter* movie.
5. We ran, jumped, and skipped acroass the schoolyard.

D. 1. My friend said, "The movie began at two o'clock."
2. We brought cookies, cakes, buns, and pies to the bake sale.
3. I don't like trying to do things that I can't do.
4. She doesn't like waiting in line at the show to buy popcorn, candy, pop, and ice cream.
5. Whenever we go shopping, we always spend too much money.
6. I will be able to stay over at your house if I finish cleaning my room.

E. 1. It's   2. our ; way
3. know ; which ; fair   4. too
5. plane ; plain   6. dye ; die
7. brake ; bear   8. Whose

F. 1. wasn't ; ever / was ; never

Grade 4 Answers

2. hasn't ; any / has ; no
3. didn't ; any
4. didn't ; anybody ; were
5. didn't ; anyone / told ; no one

15 Writing Descriptive and Narrative Paragraphs

A. (Answers will vary.)
B. (Answers will vary.)
C. (Individual writing)
D. (Individual writing)

Progress Test 2

A. 1. for ; in   2. under
   3. of   4. but
   5. until   6. with
   7. and ; or   8. over
B. 1. ADV   2. ADJ   3. ADV ; ADV
   4. ADV   5. ADV   6. ADJ
   7. ADJ   8. ADV
C. (Individual writing)
D. (Suggested answers)
   1. After we ate dinner, we watched television.
   2. Since I got a flat tire, I haven't been able to ride my bicycle.
   3. Although I slept in until noon, I was still tired.
   4. Whenever we have a picnic, it always rains.
   5. We couldn't go to the park because we didn't have a ride.
   6. We waited all day long until the bus arrived.
E. 1. complex   2. compound   3. complex
   4. complex   5. compound   6. compound
   7. compound
F. 1. Running – subject   2. dancing – object
   3. writing – object   4. Laughing – subject
   5. Swimming – subject   6. Playing – subject
   7. skiing – subject
G. 1. C   2. G   3. F   4. E
   5. H   6. B   7. D   8. A
H. 1. The grade four class memorized the poem "The Vagabond Song" by Bliss Carmen.
   2. "Scooby Doo" is a very popular children's television show.
   3. Shakespeare wrote the famous play "Romeo and Juliet".
   4. His father said, "Do not forget to take your house key with you."
   5. "What time will the movie end?" she asked.
   6. "Gulliver's Travels" is one of my favourite stories.
   7. "Think carefully before you make the decision," the teacher reminded her.
   8. One critic stated that the first "Harry Potter" book was a terrific read and a stunning first novel.

I. 1. ;   2. :   3. :
   4. ;   5. ;   6. :
J. On Canada Day, we went to Ottawa for the celebration. There were lots of people outside the Parliament Buildings. Although we were not able to get to the front, we could get a good view of the stage. The performance was superb, and everyone had a good time. "Do you want to stay for the firework display?" my father asked us. "Of course!" we all responded excitedly.
K. 1. which happened to fall on February 29 ; NR
   2. that was needed to do the job ; R
   3. who was exhausted from the race ; R
   4. who has been on staff for many years ; NR
   5. whose name was Scamp ; NR
   6. which I gave Sam for his birthday ; NR
   7. whom everyone likes ; NR
   8. who care ; R
L. (Suggested answers)
   1. We would stay at the room that was small but tidy for the night.
   2. I like the backpack which my mom bought for my tenth birthday.
   3. The game, which lasted more than four hours, was boring.
   4. The boy whom we called The Joker was funny.
   5. The tall structure which stands next to the SkyDome is the CN Tower.